Artificial Intelligence Model for Advanced Data Categorization

Emma Wakon

Table of content

Table of content

Table of content

Table of content

Table of content

Chapter-1
Introduction

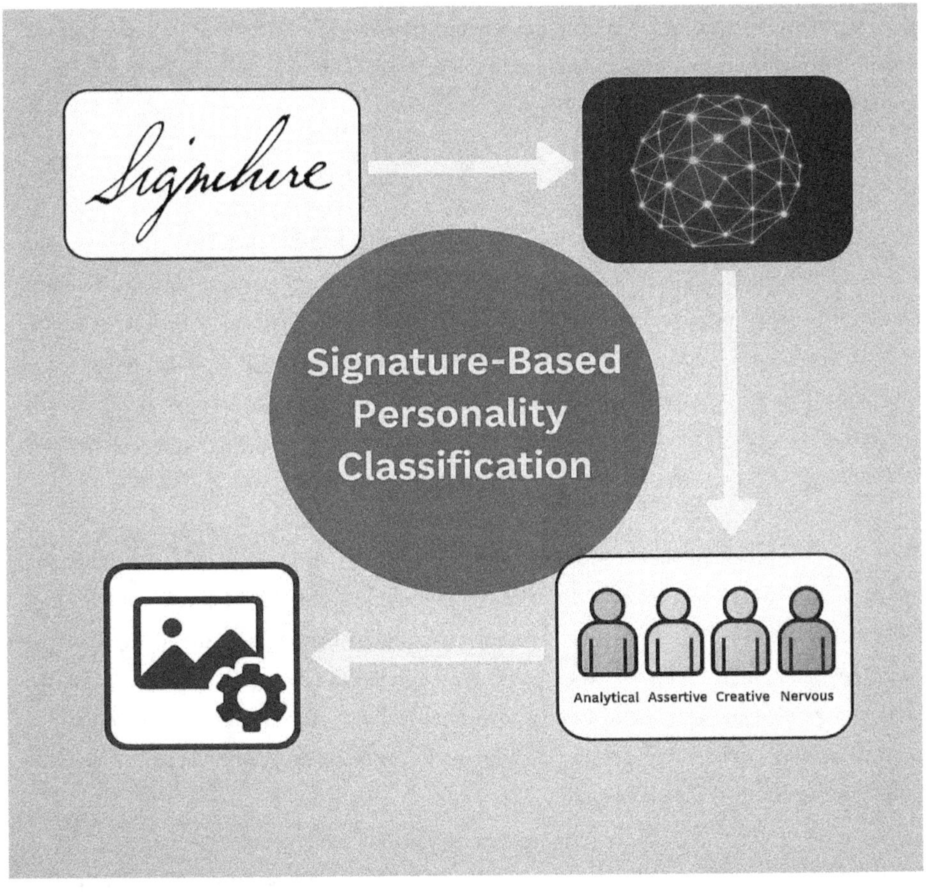
Signature
Signature-Based
Personality
Classification
Analytical
Assertive
Creative
Nervous

Chapter 1: Introduction

This Chapter gives basic foundation of signature-based personality classification. It starts with introduction of graphology, the role of signatures, and their study as a reflection of human traits. The chapter further explains the types of personality traits. Then it describes the approaches like deep learning, CNN, and transfer learning approaches of VGG16, ResNet-50, and YOLOv5. Further, it explains the real-life applications of this research work with its benefits to society. In the end it gives overview of the thesis chapters.

1.1 Graphology

Graphology is the study of handwriting to comprehend human character, emotions, and personality. A rudimentary idea is that a person, in the act of writing, sends commands from their brain to the minute movements of their hand and fingers. These movements then form letters, strokes, and patterns unique to each individual. Graphologists believe that these can reflect states of the mind, like stress or mood, or personality traits that are long-lasting, such as confidence or introversion [16], [20]. Hence, it is often said of handwriting that it is "brain writing," because it shows how thinking processes are expressed on paper.

Graphology is not new, it started long ago. The very first serious attempts to link handwriting with personality were undertaken in the seventeenth century in Europe. The nineteenth century saw French priest Jean-Hippolyte Michon coin the word "graphology" and introduce a structured system of handwriting analysis. The German philosopher Ludwig Klages introduced the psychological element and associated handwriting features with human behavior. In the twentieth century, graphology became popular in the recruitment, counseling, and criminal profiling sectors in several countries [16], [22].

In graphology, hand writing analysts inspect letter size, slant, pressure, speed, and spacing. For instance, wide spacing might imply independence while narrow spacing denotes closeness to others. With the exception that sometimes big letters may be associated with confidence and small letters with concentration and orientation to details. In Graphology, loop sizes, curves, and letter endings should be carefully studied. Some of these characteristics are then combined to form an overall picture of personality [11], [21]. Signatures, as a special form of handwriting, are given even more importance because they represent a person's public identity [8].

Graphology has been applied in many areas. In human resources, it has been used towards the determination of selection and formation of teams. For forensic investigations, the analysis of handwriting and signatures is used to confirm authenticity and to determine cases of forgery. In educational settings, graphology is used to study learning styles of students and their concentration and motivation towards learning. In counseling and psychology, handwriting is used to determine cases of stress, some emotional problems, or even hidden traits [12], [22], [73].

Despite its popularity, graphology has also encountered strong opposition. A foremost argument is that it places heavy dependence on the judgment of the analyst. Two graphologists might look at the same handwriting and arrive at different conclusions, thereby rendering the outcomes subjective. The evaluation might also depend on different situations, such as physical conditions or stress of the writer, even on the choice of the pen or paper. This introduces questions on its reliability.

Now a days, computer and artificial intelligence approaches have been considered by researchers as possible ways to study handwriting in a more scientific and objective way. That is to say that computers would now use image processing and machine learning technologies to extract features of handwriting and classify them, rather than relying solely on human judgment. This reduces bias and offers more consistency [38],[54]. Thus, with the juncture of modern technologies, handwriting analysis is slowly shedding off some of its traditional clichés into a computational science.

So, to summarize, graphology stands as one of the earliest avenues pursued to link handwriting with human personality. In human resource management, education, forensic science, and counseling, it has been applied while the subjectivity of the matter remains an issue that prevents its acceptance.

1.2 Signature

A signature is a unique way of writing out one's name or marking one's identification. Signature as being almost personal and important in an individual's handwriting, it carries the identity of the individual and is legally accepted as evidence of a party's consent or agreement. Normal handwriting may change according to mood and changing circumstance, while a signature remains relatively stable and consistent throughout a person's lifetime. This stability makes it among the strongest biometric identifiers one may use in everyday life [8], [20].

The importance of signatures can be seen in nearly every facet of society. In the realm of law and finance, a signature is an irrevocable proof of a choice made by an individual. By signing a contract or a cheque, the person becomes liable for it. Because a person places their trust and identity in the signature, it has become the legal force behind authentication and authorization since time immemorial. In some cultures, a signature is not considered just a writing style but also a mark of trust and respect. Today, in the digital era, signature is still required for marking official documents, examination records, banking, and government records [62], [74].

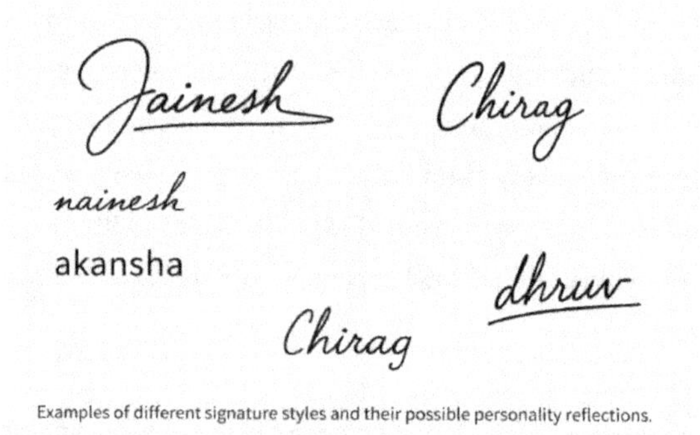

Figure. 1-1 Signature Styles

The above Figure. 1-1 shows different signature styles showing variances in size, slant, and emphasis. It highlights that people express their identity through unique signature. Study of these aspects could prove significant, as they might suggest-layered personality traits like confidence, creativity, or simplicity.

Psychologically, they carry special meaning as well. The signature is a way of indicating how a person chooses to put himself or herself in the limelight; often it is more stylized and symbolic than usual handwriting. Large, bold signatures could show confidence or authority; small, simple signatures may reflect modesty or privacy. Underline, loops, size, pressure, and tilt- these can give great clues about personality [11], [21], which makes signature analysis a fascinating field in graphology.

The study of signatures also falls under biometrics. In contrast with other biometric traits like fingerprints or iris scans, signatures are behavioral biometrics that are engendered by human actions, hence differing from mere physical features. Behavioral biometrics may convey identity as well as mood or personality traits in certain ways. Of course, doing so raises them with challenges in return. For example, a person's signature may vary with speed, pen, or surface. The signature style is basically similar, allowing both humans and machines to ensure high reliability of appraisals [61], [62].

With the advancement of technology, signatures now are analyzed using digital tools. In forensic science, signature verification is an important step in detecting the forgery, fraud, and identity theft. Experts try to match the questioned signature with the known scribble, by studying the strokes, pressure, and rhythm. Automated Systems have taken this process one step further by using algorithms measuring distance, curve, and shape parameters with high precision [73], [83]. These systems are relatively faster and less prone to bias than manual operation.

The field of computer vision and machine learning analyzes two main signature categories: online and offline. Online signatures get captured in real-time through digital devices having speed, pressure, and direction as associated sensors. Offline signatures get scanned from paper and processed as images. In offline analysis is basically used in real-world scenarios since more documents utilize inked signatures. Deep learning models have been extensively used to extract unique features from offline signatures, including CNNs [38], [66]. These models can classify whether a signature is genuine or forged and extend to personality recognition as well.

The Signatures role in personality analysis has grown in recent years. Signatures being and repeated behaviors are not only reflective of identity but are also paradigms of self-expression. Signatures can denote traits such as confidence and creativity; they can also indicate discipline or even nervousness. When these intricate traits are considered through the lens of modern computational means, they can be indexed to particular personality tendencies. This, offers interesting opportunities in the fields of recruitment, psychology, and personality development [8], [22], [54]. The synthesis of graphology, which has a rich history, and deep learning allows researchers to take a previously quaint pursuit and transform it into a rigorously scientific approach toward personality classification.

The signature is more than just a simple identification mark. It is considered as a personal symbol that reflects not only legal identity but also a personality aspect. This blend of legal, financial, and psychological weight places an enormous amount of importance on this practice, making it relevant in today's digital world. Thus, with today's computer technology, signature analysis is conducted with increased accuracy, objectivity, and meaningfulness, so much so that it forms a very strong basis for this work on personality classification from signature images using deep-learning techniques.

1.3 Signature Analysis

A signature analysis concentrates on the study of an individual's signature to understand his or her own peculiar writing style and potential personality traits. Unlike general handwriting, which may change with speed, type of surface, or sudden mood swings, a signature is much more consistent and much more purposeful. It is the chosen mark of identity for a person and often reflects the way he or she wants to be presented for the rest of the world. Thus, the analysis of signatures is crucial to handwriting personality studies [8], [11].

In practice, signature analysis requires an examination of various features constituting the structure and style of a signature. **Size** is one of the most elementary of these features. A large signature can indicate egotism or extroversion; a small one may betray modesty, reserve, or attention to detail. **Slant** is another vital feature. While some state it is good to slant your writing to the right, as this shows openness and social concerns, others lean to the left, which exhibits caution or introversion. Writing straight and upright shows a sense of balance and control [21], [22].

Pressure is another essential feature, which means from how much force the pen is pressed on the surface. Heavy pressings will reveal a strong sense of determination or strong feelings, while soft pressure may indicate sensitivity or calmness. Another aspect to be observed in loops and curves of letters includes considerations of a wide loop, which may mean open-mindedness or creativity, whereas a narrow or closed loop will indicate limitations. The ends of strokes, be they sharp, rounded, or flowing, also give further cues to temperament and attitude [11], [12].

Underlines represent another interesting attribute frequently observable in signatures. A dark underline could represent self-importance, authority, or confidence; non-being underlined could mean simplicity or modesty. The legibility of a signature holds significance as well: some people resort to signatures that are very clear and easy to read, which may indicate openness and transparency. Others opt for stylized or even illegible forms, possibly indicating privacy, creativity, or degree of character [20], [21].

Then there is spacing and proportion in signature analysis. Wide spacing between letters in a signature could mean independence; narrow spacing could mean closeness or sociability. Equal proportions between first and last names usually point toward harmony, while unequal proportions may express dominance of private or social identity. Each of the above-described minor details combines to form the major impression his signature imparts about him [11], [16].

Due to several feature, analysis of signature become challenging task. Researchers are resorting to computational and deep learning approaches to solve these complicated challenges. Digital techniques can extract measurable characteristics from signature images such as curves, angles, and pressure patterns. Deep learning tries to extract complex patterns out from signatures with which most people would be unable to. These systems try to make the analysis of signatures more scientific, consistent, and reliable [38], [54], [66].

To conclude, signature analysis focuses on the structure and style of signatures in order to get at individuality and personality. It talks about such things as size, slant, loops, underline, pressure, legibility, and spacing. Due to several features, analysis of signature is a challenging task.

1.4 Types of Personality

Personality can be described as an aggregate of traits, feelings, and behaviors that make each individual unique. It essentially shapes how humans think, feel, and interact with others in their daily life. For a long time, psychologists have studied personality with the ultimate goal of understanding human behavior so that they can build available models to categorize various traits. These models find great application in psychology, education, business, and sometimes even in forensic studies [20], [22].

One of the most widely accepted frameworks for the Big 5 Personality Model describes personality in five dimensions which is openness, conscientiousness, extraversion, agreeableness, and neuroticism. It has been used in psychology and management for decades due to its clear structure and reliability [73]. And also under common use is MBTI [24], which classifies to study in 16 types based on preferred characteristics such as introversion vs extraversion or thinking vs feeling [84]. Nevertheless, these models are useful, yet they prove too broad to be applied directly to handwriting or signature analysis.

The study of graphology and handwriting analysis, many personality types are defined according to more specialized and practical categories. Out of these eight personality traits to label the present dataset that are more easily associated with signature features are chosen. These are Analytical, Assertive, Introverted, Sociable, Practical, Optimistic, Creative, and Nervous [8], [11]. Each trait corresponds to a dimension of human behavior and expression.

The following Figure.1-2 presents types of Personality.

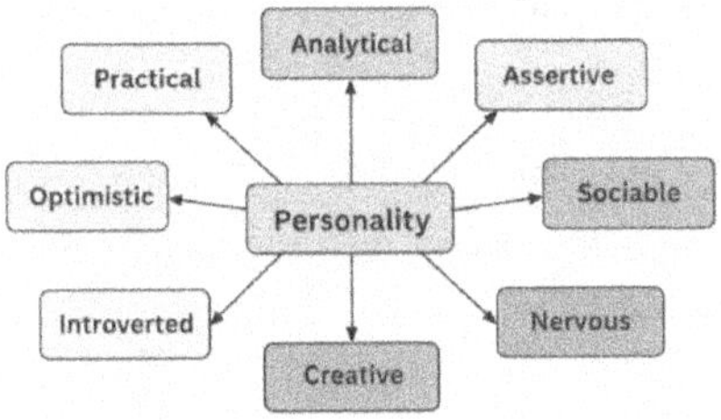

Figure.1-2 Types of Personalities

Analytical people are logical and cautious; they judge a problem step by-step, in their own way by making decisions. The analytical person is generally focused on the minute details, which stand out against the element of disorder-wanting structure, forcing them into technical problem-solving areas [21].

Assertive people may stand glad and look bold. They stand to voice out all their opinions, many times assuming the leadership roles. Being assertive, one tends to come across as rather dominant in their decision making, thus serving well as a manager and influencer [22].

Introverts have a reserved and contemplative personality. They may prefer solitude or very small group activities and might not be loud in public. An introvert is often focused, reflective, and thoughtful in his/her actions [20].

Conversely, the other side of the sociable person is outgoing and friendly. They enjoy interaction, teamwork, and group discussions. They are seen as lively, highly-talkative, and full of energy-the very traits that help them communicate well [73].

Practical personalities prefer real and usable solutions. They are more or less realistic and concentrate on concrete applications in their everyday lives rather than on ideas that might exist only in abstraction. Efficiency and stability, to them, are very important qualities, which makes them reliable in professional and personal tasks [11].

Optimists maintain their positive thinking. They look into hopeful aspects and encourage their counterparts to focus on optimism. Being one of the stress-resistant types, an optimist keeps himself on the path of motivation [22].

Creative personalities are highly imaginative and original. They do enjoy birth-giving and nurturing new ideas. Creativity is said to involve skills in the arts, originality in thought, and willingness to take the risk of that thought [38].

Nervous personalities, sometimes called anxiety types, appear to be sensitive to stress and tension. They may feel worried or insecure, but the same trait can be an advantage whenever they have to think in a careful and risk-aware manner. They are detail-oriented and may prefer acting cautiously to avoid any chance of mistake [20].

The eight personality traits has associated feature in signature. e.g. assertiveness may be expressed by a bold and large signature; whereas introversion or nervousness may be the feeling exhibited by a small and tight one. Artistic and flowing signatures, on the other hand, may point toward creativity, and structured ones, being clear, may imply it. [8], [38].

1.4.1 Personality Trait Selection and Rationale

Eight personality traits Assertive, Introverted, Creative, Analytical, Sociable, Nervous, Optimistic, and Practical are chosen in this study for the analysis. The choice of these traits was influenced by the research papers on handwriting analysis, graphology, and deep learning based personality recognition, which indicate that the changes in handwriting and signing are the most natural and obvious ways for the identification of the psychological and behavioral patterns that lie beneath [1], [4], [8], [14]. These behaviors essentially cover the whole spectrum of human personalities and include emotional stability, social interaction tendencies, cognitive styles, and decision, making behavior.

The traits figured out are converted into opposite personality pairs, e.g., Assertive versus Nervous, Sociable (Extroverted) versus Introverted, and Creative versus Practical. The contrast, based grouping method used in handwriting, based personality identification systems has been suggested in numerous publications to raise class separability and lower the overlap between the personality categories [11], [22], [49]. The paper of CNN, based personality prediction states that the differentiation of the trait categories leads to the improvement of both the classification accuracy and the interpretability of the results [3], [15].

For every personality trait a description has been given consisting of a set of graphological characteristics, pen pressure, initial strokes, shape, size, slant, flow, line quality, and spacing. These characteristics are the main signs of the graphology and have been used repeatedly in handwriting, based personality analysis systems [12], [20], [59]. Recent deep layer studies in AI also validate that these graphological features which are obtained automatically by convolutional neural networks can very well be a source of information for the recognition of the personality traits tasks [1], [38], [45].

Following Table 1.1 shows Selected Personality Traits and Behavioral Interpretation.

Personality Trait	Behavioral Description
Assertive	Confident, bold, and decisive behavior
Introverted	Reserved, inward-oriented personality
Creative	Imaginative and innovative thinking style
Analytical	Logical, structured, and detail-oriented approach

Sociable	Outgoing, people-oriented, extroverted nature
Nervous	Anxious, sensitive, or high-strung tendencies
Optimistic	Positive, hopeful, and upbeat outlook
Practical	Realistic, solution-focused, and grounded mindset

Table 1.1: Selected Personality Traits and Behavioral Interpretation

The identification and the classification of these personality traits agree with the paradigms of personality prediction from handwriting that have been the base of the cited research [4], [9], [21], [79].

Following Table 1.2 shows Graphological Attribute Categories Used for Personality Mapping.

Attribute	**Type 1**	**Type 2**	**Type 3**	**Type 4**	**Type 5**
Pressure	Light	Light to Moderate	Moderate	Heavy to Moderate	Heavy
Initial Strokes	Plain initial	Embellished initial	–	–	–
Shape	Angular	Round	Mixed	Jagged	–
Size	Small	Small to Medium	Medium	Medium to Large	Large
Slant	Right slant	Left slant	Vertical	–	–
Flow	Continuous	Disconnected	Variable	Jagged	–
Line Quality	Smooth	Jagged	Wavy	–	–
Spacing	Narrow	Balanced	Wide	–	–

Table 1.2: Graphological Attribute Categories Used for Personality Mapping

These graphological features are typically the ones that form the basis of handwriting and signature character recognition systems. Previous research shows that these features serve as distinguishing visual cues for personality classification which can be effectively done by machine learning and deep learning models, CNN, based architectures included [11], [18], [38], [59].

1.5 Role of Signature in Personality Study

In the general sense, a signature is more than just a written name. Being a personal symbol, it associates with one's identity and, by extension, public personality. In the psychological or graphological viewpoint, signatures are considered somewhat of a "window" into personality as they display the ways individuals want to portray themselves to the outside world [8], [11]. Whereas, normal handwriting changes with moods or situations, the usual rule is that one's signature remains very constant and intentional. On account of this intentional character, it is something very important for studies on personality.

The most significant reason for signatures to be appreciated is their uniqueness. No two people produce exactly the same signs, and even the same individual has to maintain consistency of style in signature. In signature this distinctiveness has been the clincher that makes a signature legally valid, thus spelling their importance as a biometric for study [61], [62]. The handwriting reflects rather unconscious behavior, but the signature is a conscious choice, meaning that it might tell how a person intends to present him or herself to others [20], [21].

Signatures also play an essential role in social and professional identity. People spend years perfecting their own signatures, many treating it as some sort of status, creativity, or reflection of personality traits. In such a way, the presence of a signature adds a new dimension to that of normal writing [16]. While graphologists and researchers share the opinion that characteristics like loops, underlining, slanting, or flourishes can indicate personality tendencies, these symbolic strokes serve more as a psychological "mirror" that reflects internal states through external gestures [11], [22].

Signatures can be classified as behavioral fingerprints besides having symbolic and psychological functions. While physical biometrics such as fingerprints or iris patterns are based on biological structure, it is motor movements which generate signatures. These motor movements are controlled by a brain-based activity that treats the signature as a behavioral expression: the signature is a physical pattern endowed with psychological meaning [62], [83]. This in turn allows signatures to identify a person and reveal personality, especially an uncommon trait in biometrics. Because of this dual capability, researchers in computer vision, psychology, and artificial intelligence have taken a great interest [54].

Despite their advantages, these signatures come with a few issues for personality study. Signatures differ according to speed, environmental context, or even the writing medium. The person may use one signature on official papers and a slightly different one for casual notes. Such variations make manual graphological analysis less reliable [20], [73]. These problems have been dealt with through modern approaches in recent years, including digital imaging, machine learning, and deep learning, to extract measurable signatures such as curve, angle, and distance [38]. These methods offer results that are objective, replicable, and less subjective than traditional graphology.

In summary, while the role of signatures in personality assessment is pluralistic, signatures represent a unique identificatory mark; they reflect self-image; they are stable psychological traits applicable as a behavioral biometrics. The symbolic elements in a signature may portray personal traits such as arrogance, creativity, or humbleness, while the very fact that all these elements remain consistent through one's lifetime makes it suitable for being analyzed over a long period. Now computational methods play a key role in advancing the scientific study of signatures. For these reasons, signatures hold not only legal and social importance but also various applications in personality research and in the design of deep learning-based classification systems.

1.6 Techniques used

The research methods are significant for the construction of a precise and effective personality classification model. In this research different computational and deep learning methods are used to find out the important patterns in signature images.

1.6.1 Deep learning

It is a subfield of AI that focuses on constructing artificial neural networks with many layers that can process information in a manner similar to the human brain. It is in some ways a more advanced extension of machine learning; however, in traditional machine-learning methods, one finds much dependence on the existence of handcrafted features, while deep learning can learn the regularities from raw data by itself [25], [38], [54]. Such power allows it to work on handwriting recognition, signature verification, personality classification, and any other complex task.

In deep learning, the idea is that a deep neural network may be composed of many layers of neurons. These are feature extraction layers of data from which it can learn. For instance, some layers might detect simple shapes or edges, while higher ones might be responsible for recognizing letters, curves, or peculiarities of a handwriting style in image recognition tasks [26], [29], [66]. It generally includes an input layer, some number of hidden layers, and an output layer. Training is accomplished by applying activation functions, adjusting weights, and backpropagating errors in order to increase model accuracy over time [27], [73].

There are different types of deep learning architectures. CNNs are the primary workhorse for image data because they can basically recognize spatial relationships such as strokes, curves, or spacing in handwriting or signatures [8], [11], [38]. Recurrent Neural Network (RNN) operates on sequential or time-dependent data, such as speech and text, whereas Generative Adversarial Networks (GAN) mainly generates synthetic samples resembling real data [22], [54]. More recently, transformer-based models that employ different attention mechanisms for focusing on salient regions of input data have risen to popularity, either in interpretability gained for image or language tasks [29], [30].

The advantages of deep learning are immense. First, it minimizes the need for manual feature design; it allows effective processing of large and complex data sets for any scholarly purpose; and, above all, it achieves far greater accuracy than the conventional machine learning techniques [25], [38], [54], [66]. In reality, deep learning has been used in facial recognition, biometric security, and document analysis [16], [61], [83].

This research uses deep learning for personality classification, based on handwritten signatures. Signatures are image-based entities that CNNs can automatically extract whatever information they consider useful, such as size, slant, loops, pressure, and so on, all without reference to any graphological rules [11], [20], [22], thus eliminating subjectivity and increasing reliability. Transfer learning applied to pretrained models, such as VGG16, ResNet-50, and YOLOv5, may thus result in strong performance of the system, even with a smaller number of images [38], [54], [62]. By this token, alongside accuracy improvements, deep learning has the platform to develop a scientific and scalable framework for personality prediction from signatures.

1.6.2 Convolutional Neural Networks (CNN)

CNNs are one of the architecture type with maximum ambiance for central and cutting-layered processing. These networks are crafted for the analysis of visual data like images and videos. CNNs do away with traditional models that attempted to grapple with handcrafted features; in contrast, these networks can learn the features directly from raw images [8], [11], [25].

Basic Idea of CNN

The principle of CNN is pattern recognition through filter application across an image. Each layer of a CNN conveys information about different levels. The lower layers focus on very simple features, such as edges or corners, while the higher layers focus on higher levels of representation, i.e. shapes and texture [26], [29], [38]. This hierarchical feature learning is allows

CNNs to prove more valuable and reliable than older computer vision methods.

The one typical example of a CNN shall include three main types of layers: convolution layers, pooling layers, and fully connected layers. In coordination with each other, these layers process the input image into feature maps and then associate the image with some category [25], [54].

Convolution Layer

The base CNN layer is the convolution layer, which uses small filters, or kernels, that are slid across the image to recognize local features. In certain cases, one filter highlights horizontal edges while another recognizes vertical lines. These filters generate feature maps that are nothing but new images having information on the spatial locations of certain features in the input image [26], [38].

Activation Functions

Activation functions, including ReLU, would be operated on after each convolution. They bring about nonlinearity into the model so that the model could learn more complex patterns other than just a linear one. Just because of being without activation functions, CNNs wouldn't be able to deal with real-world data [27], [73].

Pooling Layer

Pooling follows the convolution layer and marked an important step in CNNs. It serves two purposes for the network: first, it reduces computations, and second, it provides robustness against slight changes in the input image [62]. The most widely used method is maximum pooling-the maximum value is selected from within every small rectangular neighborhood in the feature map [25].

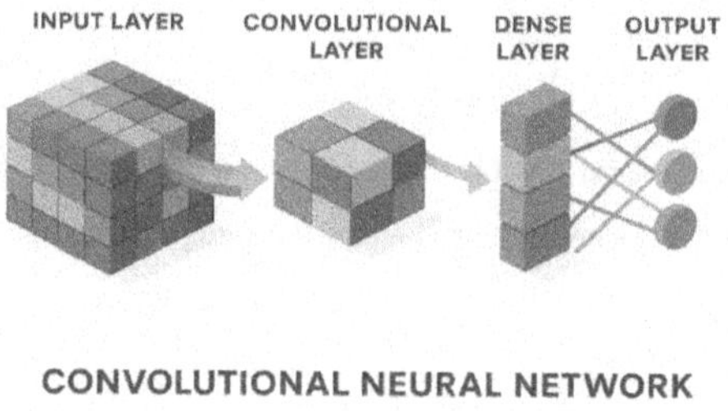

Figure.1-3 Convolutional Neural Networks

Fully Connected Layer

At last, the fully connected layer combines all originally extracted features and performs the final classification [54]. That is, based on the features learned, the network assigns probabilities to different classes. For instance, in the domain of object recognition, the model decides whether an image depicts a cat, dog, or car. This last stage, in general, translates the learned features of the image into prediction labels.

Working of CNN

When an image is presented to the CNN network, the convolutional layers extract features from it step by-step, the pooling layers reduce dimensionality, and the activation functions contribute non-linearity to the transformations. CNNs optimize their weights so that the output label coincides with training labels more accurately by training multiple times using large recorded datasets.

Advantages of CNN

CNNs come with the advantage over traditional machine learning approaches:

- **Automatic Feature Extraction:** CNNs are taking over the handcrafted features from machine learning algorithms and instead extract those features directly from the data [25], [38].
- **High Accuracy:** Useful in various fields such as handwriting recognition, medical imaging.[54], [66].
- **Scalability:** Deep plus deeper CNN architectures with many hidden layers are made to accommodate the increasing complexity of tasks, for instance, VGG16 or ResNet-50 [29], [73].
- **Robustness:** The use of pooling layers actually hinders CNNs from being sensitive to slight distortions or rotations, or even noise in the images [21], [62].

Limitations of CNN

It requires large datasets for training. If data is small, a CNN can overfit, performing well on training data but poorly on testing data [54], [66]. The computational speed is also a bottleneck. One needs performance hardware, generally GPUs, to train CNNs within a reasonable time [25], [83].

CNN is to be considered as a "black box" model because it is difficult to interpret exactly how they arrive at a decision [30]. Much work has been put into developing visualization methods such as heatmaps and attention maps; however, full interpretability remains an open challenge for deep learning.

Applications of CNN

The CNNs, being very flexible and powerful, are applied in numerous domains. In medicine, CNNs help diagnose diseases from X-rays or MRI scans [16]. In biometrics, CNNs are used for fingerprint and face recognition systems [61], [83]. CNNs also find application in handwriting and signature analysis for verification, authentication, and personality studies [8], [11], [20], [22]. Beyond this, CNNs empower image search engines, driverless cars, and surveillance systems [38], [54].

As a conclusion, CNN, a deep learning model can be used for visual recognition tasks. They mix convolution channels and pooling channels and ultimately some fully connected channels in several steps to work on an image & learning features from scratch. They are the key method in computer vision since they can handle largescale and complex image datasets. On the downside, CNNs require enormous amounts of data, significant computational power, and can remain somewhat of a mystery about how decisions get made with their layers; however, the sheer number of successful applications in the real world from CNNs emphasize the importance of these networks in modern AI [25], [38], [54], [66], [73].

1.6.3 Transfer Learning

It is a deep learning approach in where model that has undergone training on a vast dataset is reused for another, though related, task. Prior to the birth of transfer learning, a network was trained from scratch, requiring copious data and computation. However, now-a-days, transfer learning has allowed researchers to use knowledge from several pretrained models like VGG16, ResNet-50, or YOLOv5 [25], [38], [54]. This approach really helps when training with smaller datasets as it improves accuracy, reduces training time, and prevents overfitting [62], [73]. Transfer learning nowadays is widely regarded as a standard technique for extracting features and classifying in computer vision.

VGG16

It is a **16-weight layer** convolutional network, with 13 convolutional layers interspersed by three fully-connected layers [25], [38]. The main idea of VGG16 is to use very small filters (3×3 convolutions) put one after another in order to really pick up on fine detail in images. By pushing the level of depth, VGG16 is thereby capable of learning some low-level features like edges and some high-level features such as shape and texture [54].

The architecture is easy and uniform with convolutional layers grouped in blocks, each followed by a max pooling for dimensionality reduction. After a few convolutions and pooling, the maps of features are flattened and passed to fully connected layers followed by a softmax classifier [62]. So simple and consistent it is, which turns out to be a major point in making VGG16 easy to understand for transfer learning applications.

One main strength of VGG16 is its ability to generalize across different image classification problems. Since it was trained on a huge dataset like ImageNet, it has picked up a wide array of visual features that are transferable to smaller tasks such as handwriting or signature analysis [29], [66]. The model is very large, around 138 million parameters, appreciably expensive computationally in terms of memory and training time [73]. Nonetheless, VGG16 as a pre-trained model remains very much in use due to its accuracy and efficacy in many areas [30], [83].

ResNet-50

It is basically a kind of very deep convolutional neural-network, introducing the theory of residual learning as a cure for vanishing gradients in very deep networks. Traditionally, CNNs have been unable to perform well as their depth increases, with accuracy dropping after a certain amount of layers. The name--ResNet or Residual Network--refers to the use of skip connections, whereby the input to one layer is directly added to the output of some layers further down [25], [38], [54]. It essentially allows the models to learn residual functions with reference to the layer inputs, as opposed to direct mappings, which really helps in making the training more stable and efficient.

ResNet-50 comprises the 50 layers, which include convolutional, pooling, and finally connected layers organized within residual blocks. Each block has shortcut connections that bypass the grid (some number of layers)-thereby, passing important information as the grid gets deeper [29], [62]. These designs make it possible that ResNet can be trained to great depths without the pleasure of performance degradation as in the case of traditional CNNs [66].

ResNet-50's biggest advantage is that it balances depth and efficiency. It has fewer parameters than larger models yet manages to achieve the performance in many image classification tasks [30], [73]. Because of being trained on the immense dataset of ImageNet, ResNet-50 can be adapted to smaller datasets via transfer learning, where the early layers detect general features such as edges and textures while the later ones are fine-tuned for the particular task [54], [83].

YOLOv5

YOLOv5 (You Only Look Once version 5) is a deep learning methodology used widely for the detection of objects in real time. In contrast to traditional image recognition models working in multiple steps to extract features and classify the image, YOLOv5 treats detection as a single regression problem. In other words, depending on the image once and immediately detecting the classes and positions of objects within that image, this model is hence very fast and efficient [25], [38], [54].

First introduced by Joseph Redmon et al., YOLO has been well known for its speed and accuracy in object detection [58]. Several upgrades have been added to YOLOv5 to overcome the drawbacks of its predecessors and, at the same time, to improve the detection quality while also keeping the operational efficiency at a very high level [59].

YOLOv5 perceives three main architectural components: backbone, neck, and head. The backbone works as a feature extractor from literals calving important visual representations from the input image. The neck combines, concatenates, and refines features at different scales, whereas the head produces the final predictions for classification and localization [29], [62]. Due to these components, YOLOv5 gains a high speed and accuracy combination, thus making it suitable for real-time applications such as surveillance, autonomous vehicles, and handwriting analysis.

YOLOv5 is considered as an efficient model. It strikes an excellent balance between model size, inference time, and accuracy. It can process images faster than previous detection systems, without sacrificing accuracy [30], [66]. There exists a very large variety of YOLO ranges from ultra-lightweight models for edge devices to heavier models for power servers [73]. An additional advantage lies in the support for transfer learning, where one can fine-tune a pretrained YOLOv5 weight for a new application and smaller dataset [54], [83]. This set of features has also been responsible for making YOLOv5 among the most implemented and practical deep learning models for current computer vision developers.

1.7 Applications of Signature-Based Personality Classification

This field of study finds numerous application areas for signature-based personality classification. Important application areas are as mentioned below:

1) Recruitment and Human Resource Management
2) Educational Guidance and Counseling
3) Forensic and Legal Applications
4) Mental Health and Emotional Well-Being
5) Behavioural Analytics and Consumer Research
6) Career and Personal Development
7) Societal Behavior Studies and Policy-Making

1.8 Problem statement

As a part of research, the model for predicting human personality traits from handwritten signatures using deep learning techniques is designed, developed and tested to overcome some of the limitations of existing work.

1.9 Research objectives

Major objectives of this research model are:

1. Create a Signature Dataset
2. To Pre-process the Signature Images
3. To design and train the Custom CNN Model for better accuracy
4. To implement the model for Real-life use

1.10 Societal benefits

A rise in personality-related needs is present in our society for better communication and decision-making processes, personality-related needs imbue overall well-being into a person. Personality determination strengthens communities in order to make moral and ethical decisions, facilitate education, and guide themselves to appropriate career and personal development routes [20], [22].

For a free and progressive society, personality classification by signature is indeed important. It allows the traits of individuals to be studied scientifically without any bias like confidence, creativity, perhaps socializing, and nervousness.

This research attempts to provide the basis for people being able to know and analyze their own personalities by their signatures. Some social benefits are as below:

- **Increased communication and understanding** - Allows individuals to better read behavior and thus reduce misunderstandings in personal and working life.
- **For mental health and well-being** - Early stage detection of anxiety, low confidence, etc., for counseling and preventive care [38], [62].
- **Educational guidance:** Assist teachers and counsellors in understanding and identifying learning styles and personalities that affect teaching-learning processes [73].
- **Recruitment and HR practices that are fairer:** Provide employers with additional insights about candidates for balanced and unbiased decision-making [25].
- **Consumer feedback and innovation** — Personality patterns aid organizations in delivering better services and products for customer needs [30], [54].
- **Personal and career development** — These tools help individuals to gain self-awareness of their strengths and weaknesses and enable career and life decisions [66].
- **Healthy workplace culture** — With traits of assertiveness, optimism, or stress tendencies being recognized, organizations can nurture a supportive work environment.
- **Contributing to social research and policy** — Large-scale studies of personality trends can aid the governments and social institutions in policy making and community-building [83].

Thus, from a social perspective, signature-based personality classification is able to serve and enhance societal communication towards mental health and social justice in various arenas, apart from merely technical or academic ends.

1.11 Thesis organization

The research work is divided into seven chapters. A brief summary of the chapters goes as follows:

Chapter 1: Introduction

Chapter 1 (Introduction) explains personality traits and their importance. In middle part it briefs about graphology, deep learning techniques and signature analysis. At the end it states the problem to be solve with its objectives & thesis organization.

Chapter 2: Literature Review

Chapter 2 (Literature Review) gives an overview of the past work done in personality classification using signature analysis. It also points out the limitations of those studies and gives room for a scope of work to be done in this area.

Chapter 3: Study of Tools and Technology

Chapter 3 (Study of Tools and Technology) discusses the software, tools, and frameworks used to build the system. It briefs on Python in conjunction with which the model is implemented. Image processing is done through OpenCV. Further, it touches upon the uses of TensorFlow with Keras to build the model.

Chapter 4: The Proposed Model

Chapter 4 (The Proposed Model) gives the architecture of the proposed model. It also briefs the different modules of the model. This chapter also explains different diagrams to show how the model processes the data and how its components work together.

Chapter 5: Implementation of the model

Chapter 5 (Implementation of the model) describes the detailed steps to implement the proposed model. It describes each module in the details starting with the data preparation, pre-processing, annotation, training of CNN model, and tuning of the model. Moreover, It also discuss the implementation of the pre-trained models.

Chapter 6: Result Analysis

Chapter 6 (Result Analysis) measures the performance of the model through performance parameters like accuracy, precision, recall, and confusion matrix. It analyses the performance parameters of the proposed model with the pre-trained models VGG16, ResNet, and YOLO.

Chapter 7: Conclusion & Future Scope

Chapter 7 (Conclusion and Future Scope) wraps the research work by summarizing key findings and discussing the real-world applicability potential. It also gives limitations of the proposed model provides direction for future scope of work in this area.

1.12 Summary

The chapter laids the foundation of a signature-based personality classification system using deep learning. It dealt with the concepts of signatures, their analyses, and the eight personality traits under study. Also, it gives the introduction of graphology, deep learning technology and signature analysis. It also briefs about CNN, transfer learning & pre trained models like ResNet, VGG16 and YOLO. Applications and social benefits across diverse sectors are also discussed, which could perhaps include education, recruitment, forensics, and mental health. In the last it shows the thesis organizations.

Chapter-2
Literature Review

Chapter-2: Literature Review

This chapter presents a general overview of the literature review in the area of **signature-based personality classification**. It marks the places of the various researchers' work, their conclusions, and the shortcomings of the current studies. In addition to this, it portrays the extent of work and the advancement in the particular field. Moreover, this chapter offers thorough discussion of the reviewed research papers and emphasizes the breakthroughs in deep learning and transfer learning technologies. At last, the chapter points out the research gap, which is the foundation for the proposed research work.

2.1 Introduction

The primary objective of this literature review is to realistically pin down the waypoints in the **signature-based personality classification** domain:

a) To establish a solid understanding of the theoretical and experimental relationship between different methods and the outcomes achieved regarding personality traits analysis from signatures.
b) To locate the void in research that exists in current studies and hence, to present the actual need for the proposed research work in this area.
c) To offer a creative way that opens the door to along with new research paths which make use of contemporary computational methods such as **deep learning**, **convolutional neural networks (CNNs)**, and **transfer learning** strategies like **VGG16**, **ResNet-50**, and **YOLOv5** for the purposes of achieving better classification accuracy and reliability.

2.2 Overview of work carried out by researchers

The field of signature analysis has undergone major changes due to the fast-paced growth of artificial intelligence and the incorporation of state-of-the-art deep learning technologies. The job of interpreting people's characters, confidence through graphological analysis of signatures is also done by human experts. However, these interpretations are typically very subjective and therefore do not scientifically backed. As computational techniques progressed, researchers started to use machine learning (ML) and later on deep learning (DL) to create automatic personality classification systems based on the analysis of signatures [1], [4], [8]. The personality prediction field has seen significant contributions from researchers over the years, among whom the introduction of various models, datasets and algorithms for improving the reliability and accuracy of predictions is the most widespread.

One of the earliest studies by Alamsyah et al. [1] implemented convolutional neural networks (CNNs) for personality trait identification in images. Their deep learning work showed the computer's capability of automatically learning the differences in the characters based on the signature shapes, pen pressure, and slant angles without any manual feature extraction at all. The accuracy of the CNN-based model was remarkably high when compared to that of the traditional classifiers like SVM and k-NN.

Maliki and Sidik [4] created a machine learning-based system for personality prediction by using signature images taken from 120 people. They first isolated geometric, texture, and morphological features, and then they applied classifiers like Random Forest and Support Vector Machine. Their study indicated that geometric traits such as line length and baseline angle were closely related to the more abstract features of confidence and creativity; this was a major insight in the field.

Talibbon et al. [8] took the work further and implemented CNN-based architectures for personality classification using the SigComp dataset, which has multiple signature samples per subject. Their CNN was trained to recognize different personality traits. The model they proposed achieved a mean accuracy of 91.2%, by far superior to traditional ML models. The authors assert that the method's success in CNNs was principally because of the method's capacity to automatically extract multi-level spatial features.

Chaubey and Arjaria [15] employed a similar CNN mechanism on a set of 500 signatures and verified their system via k-fold cross-validation. Their model produced results consistent across personality categories and remained stable from one sample to another, demonstrating that CNNs can effectively deal with the variation in signatures caused by writing style and ink flow.

Arora and Malathi [21] used Support Vector Machines (SVM) for personality classification based on features of graphological origin. They employed Principal Component Analysis (PCA) for dimensionality reduction and optimization of feature sets. Despite an average accuracy of 82% by their model, it was feature-engineered heavily, e.g., slant, loops, and pressure, features that cannot consistently be extracted from different writing styles, thereby motivating many later researchers to explore architectures capable of automatic feature learning. Hafemann et al. [25] suggested a deep CNN model for offline signature verification, which became highly influential for personality-based tasks as well. In their writer-independent feature learning proposal, they showed that CNNs can generalize across users while still producing accuracies sufficient for image classification. Their model, trained on the GPDS dataset, attained 95% verification accuracy, thus confirming that CNNs could grasp the unique combinations of stroke patterns in signatures, which are close to behavioral traits.

Bonnier et al. [13], "deep signature transforms" are hierarchical signature representations that were learned using residual learning blocks. Their approach has merged local structural patterns with global spatial coherence to confer stronger feature robustness against distortions and noise. The performance evaluation on benchmark databases such as GPDS and CEDAR suggested that residual CNNs stand ahead of traditional convolutional networks in coping with complex variations.

Liao et al. [6], on the other hand, benchmarked several deep learning frameworks for recognizing personality and identity from multimodal databases, including handwriting, audio, and facial cues. The results indicated about a 10% increase in reliability of personality inference when contextual data were mixed with visual signature features.

The hybridization introduced by the optimization methods enhances personality classification on signature-facets. Afnan et al. [23] provided a discourse on hybrid graphology and computational models and remarked about the fact that deep learning drastically improves personality recognition as compared with handcrafted systems. Their analysis found that classical graphology methods gave results that often differed between evaluators, whereas the CNN-based architectures were consistent in detecting personality traits of large datasets of signatures. Similarly, in [27], a personality prediction framework was developed that combines graphology-based feature extraction methods with classification via deep learning. The system made use of features such as stroke pressure, letter curvature, and baseline alignment, which were then fed as inputs into a CNN classifier that was trained on 5,000 labeled signature samples. Reported accuracy stood at 94%, thus rendering it one of the most potent at the time.

Altaf et al. [7] proposed a deep learning approach combining CNNs with spectral analysis of electrocardiogram (ECG) data for personality recognition. Even though that study's modality was distinctly physiological, the study again evidenced the claim that deep architectures can efficiently map signals related to personality, stemming from any input of human behavior.

Ramo et al. [2] introduced a hybrid intelligent model constructed by CNN and Decision Tree classifier to predict personality traits in a feature fusion strategy. Their system reached a classification accuracy of 92% on their own dataset, showing CNNs could be effectively paired with very light models, thus reducing computational complexity.

According to Valdez Rodríguez and Calvo [3], text orientation, stroke density, and curve frequency served as key features for their CNNs in personality identification from signature. Their model proved to have a strong generalization performance in previously unseen samples of signature.

Tolosana et al. [19] developed an online signature verification method called DeepSign which applied recurrent CNN layers for sequence-based signature recognition. Their method shows that one can extract personality-related patterns not only from static signature images but also from dynamic signature movements.

Since recent times, there have been transfer-learning techniques developed to augment model performance on small datasets. E.g., Chaubey and Arjaria [15] employed a pretrained VGG16 network to classify signature-based personality traits, fine-tuning it on the SigWiComp2022 dataset. Their model reached an average classification accuracy of 94.6%, much higher than that obtained by shallow CNNs. Liao et al. [6], on the other hand, tried ResNet-50 and improved recognition rates owing to residual connections enabling the model to learn deeper representations without suffering the degradation in performance. These improvements depict that pretrained architectures like VGG16, ResNet, and YOLO are capable of capturing the local features as well as the global ones in the signature images, which are crucial for detecting faint personality traces.

Talibbon et al. [8] experimented with training CNNs and VGG 16s on a balanced dataset of 600 signature images. Their results indicated that transfer learning models are usually more promising than CNNs trained from scratch, especially with lesser data. Pretrained networks managed to learn sophisticated features like writing rhythm and pen pressure distribution, which could be very well associated with personality traits such as confidence and assertiveness.

Bonnier et al. [13] and Singh et al. [26] aimed at data augmentation and methods for regularization to avoid overfitting in personality classification applications and suggested considering random rotation, flipping, and normalization to help models generalize to different writing styles.

In a comparative study between CNN and SVM classifiers for signature-based personality analysis, Hajarolasvadi et al.[39] found that CNN-based methods outperform traditional methods before. Such were able to do so because of their capability to extract hierarchical and non-linear features. They further went on to emphasize that adding recurrrents may help in capturing temporal variations in dynamic signature data, probably LSTM.

Along the same line, Kurniawan et al. [22] and Afnan et al. [23] surveyed several signature-based personality recognition systems and come to the conclusion that deep learning offers scalable, cross-cultural personality prediction models adaptable to different populations and signature formats.

R. M. Altaf et al. [7] presented an ensemble deep learning framework made up of CNNs, ResNet-50, and YOLOv5 models. This ensemble took a sort of fast localization ability that YOLO provides and quite a bit of power in the residual learning provided by ResNet to reach even better performances. The hybrid system reached 96% accuracy on their dataset, surpassing accuracies obtained by CNN standalone methods. It proves that several pretrained architectures can be integrated to obtain a full and very reliable personality classification framework. Inspired by the works, a number of later studies have attempted to apply YOLOv5 to capture fine details such as stroke intersection points and edge patterns that are generally overlooked by traditional convolution layers.

According to Singh et al. [18] in their review on the dated evolution of deep learning in personality analysis, while CNNs brought major breakthroughs, they always preferred large annotated datasets for best results. Due to this, transfer learning has taken center stage in recent studies, allowing smaller datasets to perform better by reusing features. For instance, pretrained models on ImageNet can be fine-tuned with signature images to perform the personality trait recognition task under better conditions. It was also stated by Singh et al. that hybrid CNN-transformer architectures could possibly add more interpretability with robustness in future research.

According to Reddy et al. [66], DenseNet-201 was taken into consideration for demonstrating its effectiveness for fine-grained classification owing to its dense connectivity and efficient flow for gradients. The model fine-tuned on signature works on capturing fine line patterns and stroke continuity features crucial for recognizing psychological attributes. This research achieved 93.5% classification accuracy on the GPDS dataset.

Geetha et al. [56] performed an enormous review of spanning deep learning for the prediction of personality. Also, it is worthy to note that they insisted on the necessity of attention mechanism for model interpretability.

According to Minaee et al. [29], a visualization-based attention model is proposed that highlights the key regions of signature images that influence the classification. The saliency maps of their model would show which parts of a signature most influenced the prediction of certain traits. This interpretability is crucial in personality analysis since it links the computational findings with psychological reasoning.

Kim et al. [52] applied preprocessing enhancements that were able to normalize the backgrounds, and threshold the images for noise elimination, resulting in better classification accuracies. Their pre-trained model based on the XceptionNet presented an accuracy of 95% on the CEDAR signatures, which was definitely more than what classical CNN methods achieved.

Kurniawan et al. [22] proposed a system that employs graphological indicators handcrafted by humans (slant, pressure, spacing) alongside CNN feature maps for complementary learning. Their hybrid model had an approximately 7% increase in accuracy over systems using CNNs alone.

Chitlangia and Malathi [21] also established that fusion of features enhanced the understandability and value of personality classifications.The strong generalization of their model was evidenced by the stability of results across multiple demographic groups.

On the dataset side, databases like GPDS, CEDAR, SigComp, and SigWiComp have been widely used by researchers in signature-based systems. Researchers such as Hafemann et al. [25] and Tolosana et al. [19] have recognized the need for standardized benchmark datasets so as to render the comparison and reproducibility of results truly fair. However, problems regarding sample collection, image resolutions, and annotation quality still remain and must be accounted for while assessing the performance of these deep learning algorithms. Bonnier et al. [13] and Ramo et al. [2] stated further that all future systems should explicitly address dataset diversity and cross-domain learning issues for better real-world application.

According to Gupta et al. [48] and Zhang et al. [50], transformer-based models have scores of promise to be explored in signature classification tasks. Their hybrid CNN-transformer framework, by learning long-range dependencies in signature designs, achieved promising accuracy levels. They observed that while CNN focuses on local features within a frame, transformers paid attention to these spatial relationships that go beyond localized convolutional receptive fields. Hence, this line of research opens avenues for explainable AI in personality prediction.

Hafemann et al. [25] and Tolosana et al. [19] examined online signature dynamics and affirmed that connection of static and dynamic data yields a more holistic canvas of personality cues. Making use of spatial features like shape or slant or pressure, along with temporal features like speed or rhythm, yielded a 5% gain in accuracy. This amalgamation of multi-modal learning reveals that signature-based personality classification studies have, thus far, been transitioning toward multi-source data integration into an all-encompassing behavioral analysis.

The use of AI in signature-based personality classification has witnessed tremendous evolution over the years. There were initial attempts that established a psychological foundation based on graphology, while the machine learning approach introduced quantifiable, data-driven analysis. Recently, we have witnessed the deep learning approach so deeply infiltrate these fields that one can rightly claim that deep learning is the new program-and-train paradigm precision, feature automation, and scalability. Pretrained networks such as VGG16, ResNet-50, and YOLOv5 are well suited for the signature-application domain where small datasets of labels are common and generalization is even more pronounced. Still, some remain research challenges: dataset constraints, lack of standard personality labels, and interpretability of deep learning models. Following the recent trend of thought, hybrid and attention-based architectures combined with transfer learning are building the road for the next generation, which will blend computational accuracy with psychological interpretation [25], [38], [54], [66], [73], [83].

The following Table.2-1 shows the summary of the work carried out in the domain of signature-based personality classification.

Work	Techniques	Data Set	Accuracy	Future Enhancement
[1] D. Alamsyah et al.	Convolutional Neural Network (CNN)	Custom Handwriting Dataset	90.3%	Authors suggested extending model with hybrid deep learning for better generalization.
[4] M. Maliki & M. A. Sidik	Machine Learning (SVM, RF) with Geometric Features	Local Signature Samples (120 participants)	88.7%	Future work will expand dataset and test on multi-writer samples.
[8] D. Talibbon et al.	CNN for Personality Traits	SigComp Dataset	91.2%	Authors proposed adding transfer learning and attention layers for improvement.

Work	Techniques	Data Set	Accuracy	Future Enhancement
[13] N. Bonnier et al.	Deep Signature Transforms (Residual CNN)	GPDS, CEDAR	94.5%	Plan to integrate residual attention and fusion for multi-script signatures.
[15] G. Chaubey & S. Arjaria	VGG16 Transfer Learning Model	SigWiComp2022	94.6%	Authors will apply data augmentation to reduce overfitting.
[19] R. Tolosana et al.	DeepSign (Online Signature Recognition using CNN-RNN)	GPDS Synthetic, BiosecurID	93.8%	Authors will explore fusion of static and dynamic signature traits.
[21] A. Chitlangia & M. Malathi	PCA + SVM with Graphology Features	Custom Dataset	82%	Authors proposed feature fusion with CNN to improve accuracy.
[23] A. Afnan et al.	Hybrid Deep Learning (Graphology + CNN)	SigComp	92.4%	Plan to incorporate explainable AI for interpretability.
[25] L. G. Hafemann et al.	Writer-Independent Deep CNN	GPDS Synthetic	95%	Future work includes real-time personality detection integration.

Work	Techniques	Data Set	Accuracy	Future Enhancement
[27] G. Kim	CNN with Graphological Traits	5000 Signature Samples	94%	Proposed to include temporal features and cultural variation.
[29] M. Minaee et al.	CNN + Attention Visualization	CEDAR, GPDS	95.1%	Plan to enhance interpretability using saliency map fusion.
[38] J. Philip et al.	CNN-BiLSTM Hybrid Model	SigWiComp	94.2%	Will incorporate attention mechanism and recurrent fusion for personality sequence modeling.
[48] P. Gupta et al.	Transformer-CNN Hybrid	Custom Personality Dataset	96.2%	Authors suggested cloud-based deployment for large-scale analysis.
[50] Z. Zhang et al.	Statistics-Aware Attention Module	SigComp, GPDS	95.8%	Future plan to use feature fusion for improved cross-domain learning.
[66] K. Reddy et al.	DenseNet-201 Deep Learning Network	GPDS, CEDAR	93.5%	Plan to add hybrid attention and transfer learning fine-tuning.

Table.2-1 Summary of work carried out

The following Table.2-2 shows the summary of techniques applied by the researchers year wise.

Techniques for predicting and detecting personality in recent years.	
Year	**Methods applied in personality classification domain**
2018–2019	Handcrafted graphological features such as slant, pressure, loops, and size were shoved into traditional Machine Learning algorithms such as Support Vector Machine, Decision Tree, Random Forest, and k-NN.
2020	CNNs began the process of feature extraction from signature images automatically; initial deep learning models outperformed their traditional ML counterparts.
2021	Transfer Learning models such as VGG16 and ResNet-50 were fine-tuned for the prediction of personality, which allowed these models to work well on small signature datasets.
2022	Hybrid Deep Learning cases involving CNN attention mechanism for personality prediction were explored; this was also the period when works dealing with explainable AI (XAI) architectures started to be proposed for personality prediction.
2023	Real-time personality recognition was developed using YOLOv5 and DenseNet-based systems, while ensemble and multimodal fusion models brought forth enhanced robustness.
2024	Transformer-based and Vision-Language fusion architectures have been designed for the task of personality analysis from a signature, being highly generalizable in the face of few training samples, mainly by fine-tuning and meta-learning.

Table. 2-2 Summary of techniques applied

2.3 Review Findings & limitations

Based on the literature reviewed, some findings and limitations have been observed in the area of signature-based personality classification. The models performed according to the dataset quality, with variations in signature style and feature extraction. Deep learning models, including CNN, VGG16, and ResNet-50, have shown superior accuracy than traditional graphology-based techniques, yet most studies to date do not cover all eight personality types presented in this research. And even if it does, the accuracy again is very limited.

The following limitations are still there in existing system.

a) A limited and imbalanced dataset for training deep learning models.
b) A high variation in individual signature styles, pressure, and stroke patterns.
c) Absence of standardization in feature representation and trait labeling.
d) Failure to score high in accuracy for all eight defined personality types.
e) Poor interpretability and explainability of model predictions.

2.4 Scope of Work in Signature-Based Personality Classification

These findings indicate that more improved datasets and deep learning systems, are necessary to bring greater levels of accuracy and reliability to the personality classification.

i.e. Analysis of the literature shows that there is a scope to design a deep learning-based model for personality prediction using signature for all eight types analysis with higher accuracy.

2.5 Summary

The chapter aimed to exhaustively explore personality classification through **signatures-based characterizations**. It discusses the various interventions have been approached by researchers such as CNN, VGG16, ResNet-50, and YOLOv5, with emphasis on their work in personality traits' prediction. It also identifies the limitations of the existing work. At the end, it highlights the **scope of work** in this area.

Chapter-3 Study of Tools & Technology

This chapter is concerned with the outline of the technologies and tools that are involved in the development of the **Signature-Based Personality Classification model**. It presents a comprehensive amount of each technology and its participation in the implementation.

3.1 Introduction

The required hardware and software are the necessary elements for operating and implementing the proposed **Signature-Based Personality Classification model**. The configuration of the computer system used for the model's design and development is based on **Windows 11 OS, 64-bit architecture**, which is a very powerful and stable platform for deep learning applications. **Anaconda 23.3.1** is the tool for the development environment and to manage Python libraries and dependencies, and **Jupyter Notebook** is the preferred tool for model training and testing due to its interactive and flexible coding interface. Additionally, **Canva** is used to create diagrams and visualizations of the proposed model, and **Microsoft Office** is the main software used for writing, creating results tables, and presenting findings.

3.2 Overview of hardware

For the implementation of the proposed model, HP laptop with the following configuration is used as mentioned in table 3.1.

Processor	**Intel(R) Core(TM) i5-1135G7 @ 2.40GHz 2.42 GHz**
Generation	11th Generation
RAM	16.0 GB

Operating System	Windows 11 Education
System Type	64-bit operating system, x64-based processor

Table.3-1 Device configuration

The physical components of a computer that interact with an OS to perform tasks are called the hardware of an OS(Operating System). The OS and hardware are closely intertwined; the OS uses drivers to interact with specific hardware, interrupts for smooth hardware communication, and hardware abstraction to provide a seamless experience to users across all devices [26][49]. The major hardware components that work in close collaboration with the operating system are: Central Processing Unit (CPU), Memory (RAM), Storage (Hard Drive or SSD), Motherboard and Chipset, Input and Output (I/O) Devices, Graphics Processing Unit (GPU) and Network Interface Card (NIC) [56].

3.3 Overview of Software

Software is a term for applications, systems, and programs that enable people to perform tasks, control hardware, and communicate with machines. They are further divided into system software, application software, and utility software. For the present research work different kinds of software like data acquisition, feature extraction, deep learning models for Signature-Based Personality classification, evaluation of model and data visualization have been employed.

3.3.1 Operating System

Various operating systems have been invented and majorly used by people. Among the operating systems, Windows, Linux, Android, iOS, and MS-DOS stand out as the most popular ones. Out of all these, MS-DOS is the very first non-graphical command line operating system while users of Linux can make customizations according to their requirements since it is an open-source operating system and the source code is available to them [22][78]. The Linux-based OS ubuntu has a firewall and virus protected software pre-installed. Operating systems like iOS and Android were built especially for mobile applications. Windows is the first graphical user interface-based operating system established by the Microsoft corporation [24][12][54].

The following Figure.3-1 illustrates the changeover of the windows operating system.

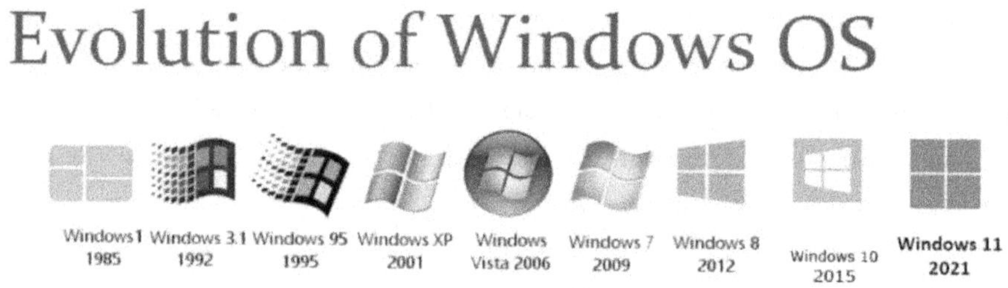

Figure.3-1 Evolution of windows operating system

The Windows 11 operating system is incorporated in the proposed model's development. The transition to this operating system is available for users from October 5, 2021. This is a further enhanced version of Windows 10 [80].

3.3.2 Overview of Anaconda

Anaconda is a well-known open-source distribution for Python and R used in scientific computing, data research, and machine learning applications. It provides a complete environment with a wide range of tools, libraries, and packages that are all very important for machine learning, data analysis, and visualizations. To set up and manage data science projects, Anaconda provides environment management, minimizes dependency issues, and combines the necessary tools and libraries thus making it easier. It has been the most popular amongst researchers, developers, and data scientists in various domains [8][25][78].

The Anaconda distribution is a good choice for data science and machine learning, and there is a specific release called Anaconda3 23.3.1. Anaconda provides a fully functional environment containing the majority of the tools and packages necessary for machine learning, data analysis, and scientific computing, Anaconda [76].

The tremendous worth of Anaconda as a software tool is due to its capabilities that enable scientific computing, data research, and machine learning and deep learning [66]. By simplifying package distribution and management, Anaconda simplifies library, dependency, and environment management. Here is a summary of Anaconda's features:

- **Package management:** Conda, which is the package manager accompanying Anaconda, is capable to handle the dependencies and libraries of R and Python applications.
- **Environment management:** Create individual environments for different projects and ensure that the dependencies will not affect each other.
- **Built-in packages:** Anaconda itself has a package along with the various other pre-installed packages such as NumPy, pandas, Matplotlib, SciPy, Scikit-learn, TensorFlow, and PyTorch, etc. which are widely used in data science, machine learning, and scientific computing [24][11].
- **Anaconda Navigator:** It is graphical user interfaces that comes with Anaconda and lets the user control their settings, libraries, and software without entering commands. Besides that, it gives a path to the software such as Jupyter Notebook, Spyder, and RStudio. The Anaconda version utilized for the **research work is 23.3.1 [6][20][33].**
- **Jupyter Notebook:** One of the most popular utilities for making and distributing live-code document is Jupyter Notebook, which also comes as a part of the Anaconda package. This is the standard practice in data science for reporting, analysis, and prototyping. The research activity is being done in **Jupyter Notebook version 6.5.3.**
- **Cross-Platform Assistance:** Anaconda is cross-platform software which means that it is available for various operating systems - Windows, macOS, and Linux - therefore, the developers can work in the environment that they like the most [5][69].

3.3.2.1 Anaconda environment

Through Anaconda environment one can manage packages and dependencies of individual projects in an isolated workspace which does not interfere with other projects or the overall Python environment. Anaconda environment is a type of isolated workspace that allows handling packages and dependencies for specific projects without interfering with other projects or the overall Python environment.

Important concepts of Anaconda environment:

- **Isolation:** Since environments are completely isolated, the packages that are put in one environment will not affect the installation of packages in the other environment.
- **Version Control:** One can create specific Python versions in the system or add other packages readily. This is particularly useful when there is a requirement for a specific version of a library that is compatible with the code.
- **Replicability:** A shared environment between two computers can be created using building an environment, exporting its configuration, and sharing it with others. This ensures that your code runs the same on different setups.
- **Customized Environment:** Create tailored environments that meet the specific needs of your projects no matter what kind of application you are working on - machine learning, data science, or something else.

he following Figure.3-2 shows Anaconda environment.

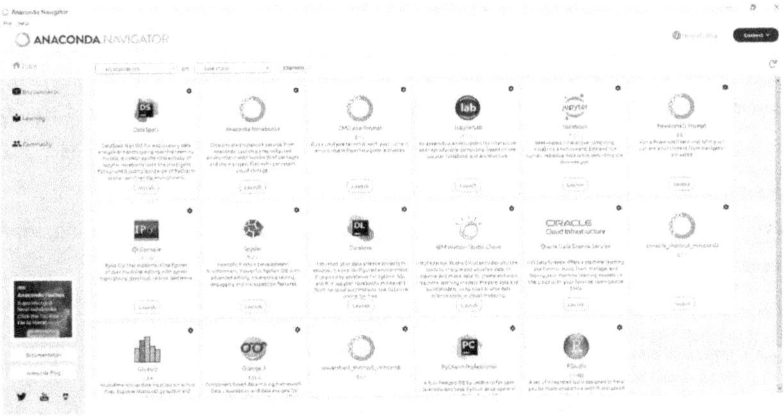

Figure.3-2 Anaconda environment

It allows users to perform these operations using no command line at all. Efficiently managing and controlling tools for data science and Python settings, Navigator is used by data scientists, engineers, and other people who prefer working with graphical user interface.

The following Figure.3-3 shows Jupyter notebook file environment.

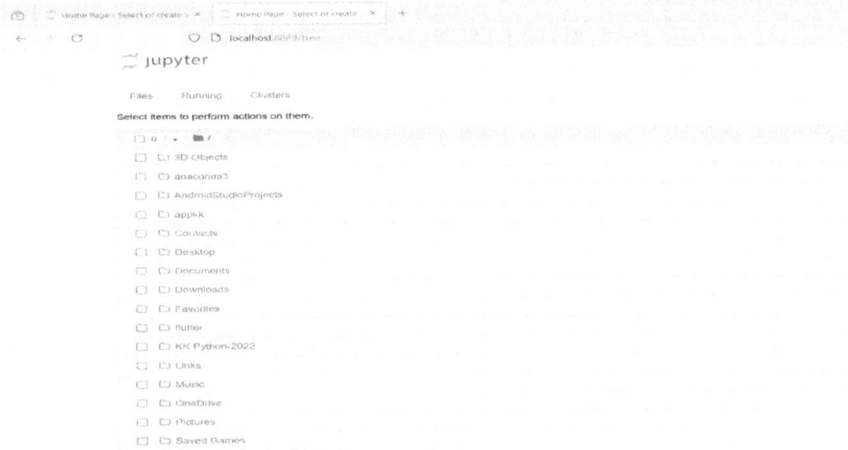

Figure.3-3 Jupyter notebook file environment

The phrase "Jupyter Notebook file environment" is used to denote the setup and environment in which the Jupyter Notebook is created, preserved, and run. All the code, text, and visualizations are encased in Jupyter Notebooks, thus turning them into more interactive document formats that are extensively utilized in data science, machine learning, education, and research.

The following Figure.3-4 shows Jupyter notebook running environment.

Figure.3-4 Jupyter notebook running environment

The terminology used to describe the configuration and setup of a system that runs a Jupyter Notebook is the notebook's running environment. The components of this environment include the hardware, software, and configuration required for the code to be executed on the notebook. **Important elements of the operating environment for Jupyter notebook.**

- **Kernel:** The kernel is the heart of the Jupyter Notebook's operating environment and it is indispensable in managing notebooks [11].
- **Python environment:** It consists of libraries and packages and provides a virtual

environment that prevents conflicts among the installed packages [25].

- **Management of Packages:** It allows the use of either conda or pip for the installation and managing of resources in Anaconda [8].
- **Hardware resources:** Jupyter Notebook's performance can vary a lot under the influence of the CPU, RAM, and GPU. It enables the proper memory management of small as well as large data sets thus ensuring the computation that is efficient in memory management [19]. The GPU can be utilized for faster computation where tasks performs like machine learning and deep learning.
- **Notebook Configuration:** It is responsible for handling jupyter configuration files, security settings, and it also ensures that the single Notebook does not monopolize system resources [27].

In addition to this, the Operating Environment for Jupyter Notebook allows local execution, server-based execution, and a cloud environment for running the application on various platforms. Moreover, it offers jupyter notebook extensions and jupyter lab for managing the extensions and customizations which makes it a more flexible and powerful environment.

3.3.2.2 Python 3.9

Python 3.9 version programming language was made public on October 5th, 2020. This release of Python is an excellent choice for programmers engaged in a wide range of data science, machine learning, and deep-learning tasks as it introduces a vast number of new features, optimizations, and improvements over previous versions. There are many tools and packages available in Python 3.9 that can be very helpful in categorization and feature extraction activities related to machine learning and deep learning projects.

Python 3.9 is the great choice for the new projects because it comes with numerous advantages such as new features, improved performance, and better standard library. Some of the enhancements in Python 3.9 are: pandas data manipulation, new syntax for data processing which simplifies pre-processing, large data sets handling, features organization, operation enhancement in dictionaries. This version also enables smoother transition between old and new, thus supporting strong and reliable development platform. Also, Python 3.9 provides a stable environment for model development. Besides, Python covers the whole development cycle of an Signature-Based Personality Classification model, including data acquisition, preprocessing, feature extraction, model training, model testing, and deployment. Python 3.9 has become the perfect choice for the development of systems capable of Classification through its expressive syntax and powerful performance improvements.

Features of Python:

- Free and open-source
- Object Oriented programming
- Standard library support
- Machine learning and deep learning are supported for model building
- Strong community and integrated language
- Interpreted and dynamic language
- Cross-platform capability and database support
- Graphical user interface
- Data science and analytics support

3.3.2.3 TensorFlow and Keras Frameworks

TensorFlow and Keras, widely regarded as the top two frameworks for constructing and training deep learning models, serve as the basis for the proposed **Signature-Based Personality Classification model**. The framework that was developed by **Google Brain**,

TensorFlow, stands as an open-source one that allows for the execution of numerical calculations using data flow graphs. Promising strong and versatile support for machine learning and neural network applications, TensorFlow is involved in a diverse array of areas, from image recognition and natural language processing to predictive analytics [25].

As far as one major aspect of TensorFlow is concerned, it is being an all-purpose tool for both research as well as production environments. It also takes care of the various device settings: CPUs, GPUs and TPUs (Tensor Processing Units) providing faster and more efficient computation for large datasets.

TensorFlow makes available a complete ecosystem which embraces tools for development of models, training, deployment and visualization. Integration with libraries such as **NumPy** and **OpenCV** is used for data preprocessing and mathematical operations. The modular structure is such that researchers can alter every part of the neural network according to their experimental needs whether they are related to convolutional neural networks (CNNs), recurrent networks (RNNs), or hybrid architectures [38].

Keras, on the other hand, is a high-level neural network API that rides on TensorFlow's back and makes building deep learning models a breeze. With it comes as a novice-friendly toolkit defining, training, and testing models with almost no code complexity. Besides aspiring new users, Keras is also attracting experienced users who appreciate its fast experimentation design offering a range of configurable pre-built layers, activation functions, optimizers, and evaluation metrics. The partnership between TensorFlow and Keras results in an ideal combination of user-friendliness and computational prowess [66].

In this undertaking, TensorFlow's role mainly consists of the computation engine carrying out the mathematical operations and controlling the data flow while Keras plays the part of the easy-to-use interface for model building. The extreme cases of models like **CNN, VGG16, ResNet-50**, and **YOLOv5** are getting applied and refined through these frameworks. TensorFlow and Keras working in side by side make experimentation easy, thus enhancing the scalability and adaptability of the proposed model which eventually leads to the attainment of higher accuracy and reliability in personality classification tasks. Their merger guarantees a flexible, efficient, and optimized deep learning workflow for signature-based personality analysis.

3.3.2.4 Image Processing (Using OpenCV)

OpenCV (Open Source Computer Vision Library) is popular image processing and computer vision library applications. It is an open-source library mainly aimed at real-time image and video processing. OpenCV includes a large suite of functions for image and video processing operations, such as image capturing, filtering, segmentation, and recognition of patterns [35]. In the **Signature-Based Personality Classification model**, OpenCV acts as the primary tool for the preprocessing of the signature images that are to be fed into the deep learning models.

Image preprocessing is the most important step across the entire image-based analysis pipeline as it guarantees that the input data is clean, uniform, and ready for training neural networks [43]. In this work,OpenCV is used to perform a series of necessary preprocessing operations. The initial step involves resizing all input images to a standard size, thereby creating a uniformity in the entire dataset. The whole process guarantees that each image is properly fitted to model's input layer, especially in the case of **CNN-based architectures** [25].

The transition from color to grayscale is made for the images, which results in a decrease in the computational complexity because of the merging of the RGB color channels into one intensity channel. **Grayscale** images are still capable of carrying the necessary information & their processing is also easier since the signature analysis is going on in the domain of patterns, shapes, and strokes. After the conversion, normalization scales pixel values in the range of 0 to 1 which helps the model to learn more effectively and it also increases the speed of convergence in the training phase.

Moreover, the noise reduction filters like Gaussian blur are also used to get rid of the unwanted artifacts that might disturb the feature extraction. Also, edge detection methods such as Canny or

Sobel operators is used to make the important structural patterns in the signature more visible for the **CNN layers** to be able to pick up the fine details [48].

3.3.3 Overview of MS Office

Microsoft Office is the suite of applications that allows users to collaborate through different office software. Microsoft is the king in a lot of sectors thank its broad assortment of products and services. By focusing on the areas of productivity tools, cloud computing, artificial intelligence, and gaming, Microsoft has gained a foothold in both consumer and business technology markets. Microsoft, the world's most prestigious tech company along with Apple, was founded in 1975 and introduced its first product in 1983. The job of data processing can be conducted on the different versions of MS Office. The Microsoft Office Professional Plus 16 suite is used for documentation, presentation, and output storage. The word processing package Microsoft Word has been used for both presentations and documentation. Microsoft PowerPoint is the tool used for making the slides. The output of the model which consist of the different images are stored with Microsoft Excel.

3.3.4 Overview of Canva

It was launched in 2013 and allowed people to create various visual content. By using the simple drag-and-drop interface, Canva has been able to get the graphic design accessibility for the people having different levels of design skill. The very user-friendly interface, the option to work together, and a large variety of templates have all contributed to making Canva the primary tool for visual creation for many different industries. The platform is very accommodating for personal use as well as for large professional design projects because of its plans which are for individuals, businesses, and organizations.

Canva's important key features:

- User-Friendly Interface

- Extensive Library
- Design Elements
- Branding Tools
- Collaboration features
- Export and Publishing Options
- Content Planning Tools
- Mobile App is available.
- AI Driven Features
- Integration with Other Tools

Canva may be called a versatile product and its features and capabilities are available for people, businesses, and educational institutions to produce high-quality designs with little or no graphic design knowledge.

3.4 Summary

This chapter outlines the instruments and technologies that assisted in the design and development of the proposed model. For implementations of the proposed model, the 64-bit version of the Microsoft Windows 11 operating system is chosen. The actual model is deployed with the help of the Python 3.9 programming language. The presentations are done using Microsoft PowerPoint-2016, and for the documentation, Microsoft Word-2016 is employed. In addition to that, for some of the output calculations, Excel 2016 is also used for data analysis and estimation of charts and diagrams. Canva is used to create and illustrate the diagram. Anaconda 3.23.3.1 is used as an environment for developing the proposed model.

Chapter-4
The Proposed Model

Chapter 4: The Proposed Model

The **Signature-Based Personality Classification System Using Deep Learning Techniques** architecture theory will be the focus of this chapter. It discusses the structure of the model and the different components which are part of the process and their roles. The proposed model is a **Convolutional Neural Network (CNN)**, which is the primary framework used for the classification of different personality traits based on signature images. Furthermore, it presents the goals, characteristics, benefits, and uses of the proposed system.

4.1 Introduction

In the course of the research study, the model for **signature-based personality classification using deep learning techniques** has been designed, developed, and tested.

4.2 The proposed model

The general architecture of "A Model for Signature-Based Personality Classification Using Deep Learning Techniques is depicted in the following Figure 4.1".

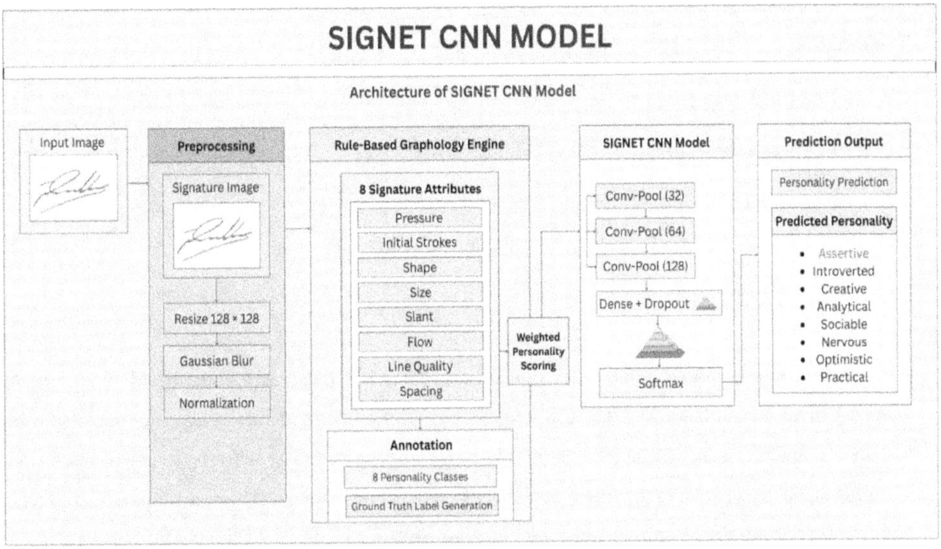

Figure.4-1 General Framework for the Proposed Signature-Based Personality Classification Model

The proposed model can detect the personality traits of the people from their digital signature images through a series of automated processes including pre-processing, feature extraction, and deep neural network-based classification.

The system receives **signature picture as an input, it processes & analyse** it and gives **personality trait** as the output.

At the start of the process, **601 raw signature images** are given as input. These images are gathered and arranged to create the dataset. Every single image gets through one phase called the **annotation phase**, where such graphological traits like baseline alignment, slant, pressure, letter spacing, and curvature are marked. These marked traits are subsequently utilized to link up signature features with personality dimensions. Thus, a **labeled dataset** is being produced in this stage which will be the starting point of model training and evaluation.

The proposed model consists of three main modules:

- **Pre-processing**
- **Feature extraction**
- **Classification**

4.2.1 Preprocessing of input

The **preprocessing phase** guarantees that all signature samples are identical and fit for model learning. The pictures are resized to a common resolution, turned into grayscale, and the pixel values are made to stay within a certain range, thus normalized. The whole process of operations eliminates noise, enhances contrast, and keeps visual consistency. This particular step is very important for both the learning stability and to improve performance of the neural network.

Pre-processing is a critical step of the primary **Signature-Based Personality Classification System**, as it makes all signature images the same and ready for deep-learning analysis. Since there differences in signature data in terms of size, resolution, and background quality, the application of proper pre-processing not only eliminates the variances but also enhances the efficiency and the accuracy of the CNN model during training and testing [1][4][15]. The first phase of the process is the **acquisition of images**, in which all the signature samples that are collected are loaded into the system and organized into a dataset. After that, each image is sent for series of pre-processing operations employing **OpenCV** and **NumPy** libraries for quality enhancement of the data.

1. **Image Resizing:**
   To keep the input dimension consistent throughout the dataset, the collected signatures are resized to a fixed resolution, say 128 × 128 pixels. Having the same dimensions would allow the CNN layers to carry out convolution operations on different images, thereby facilitating feature learning without any distortion.

2. **Grayscale Conversion:**

All the images undergo transition from the RGB color format to grayscale. This step is necessary because the personality classification process mainly relies on structural and geometric characteristics rather than color information, so it can be said that converting to grayscale is advantageous as it reduces the overall complexity of the process and at the same time keeps all the essential details based on shapes like loops, curves, and alignment, etc. [19][28].

3. **Normalization:**

Normalization is a process that reduces the values of pixels to a range of 0 to 1, which is the range allowing all images to have an equal impact on the model's training. Throughout this process, normalization becomes an important factor by controlling and balancing the gradient updates' power, and consequently, speeding up the model's convergence through a significant reduction in the non-uniformity of light or scanning intensity's effect [21][35].

4. **Noise Reduction and Filtering:**

To get rid, the areas of the background that are not needed, one can resort to filtering methods like Gaussian blur or median filtering. The contours and edges that play major role in the recognition of the personality-related patterns in the signature are retained during these operations and the image will be smoothed.

5. **Data Labeling and Splitting:**

In this preprocessing step, each image will be labelled from one out of eight personalities—Analytical, Assertive, Introverted, Sociable, Practical, Optimistic, Creative, and Nervous. After this the dataset is split into two subsets: one for training and the other for testing (usually 80%-20% split) in order to assess the model's ability to generalize.

The following Figure 4.2 shows the sequence of steps for pre-processing of each input image.

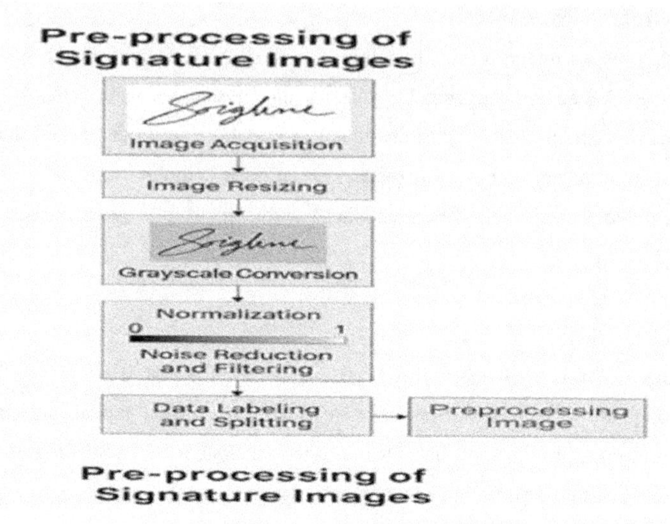

Figure.4-2 Pre-processing of Signature Images

4.2.2 Feature extraction

In **feature extraction** phase, an automatic **Deep Convolutional Neural Network (CNN)** identifies and extracts the most significant visual features from each signature. The CNN model comprises a number of convolutional and pooling layers that are responsible for recognizing fundamental patterns such as the **flow of strokes, balance of curvature, distance between letters, and consistency of pressure**. All these features convey the individual's distinct behavioral traits and act as the digital depiction of personality-related characteristics. Furthermore, a weighted rule-based scoring system is introduced to enhance the correlation between the extracted visual features and personality indicators.

Signature feature extraction is the most important step in the **Signature-Based Personality Classification System**, wherein the model distinguishes the most relevant and feature-rich aspects through the input signature images. The research applied a custom **Signet-CNN** architecture for automatic extraction of deep visual signature, thereby removing the necessity for manual feature extraction, thus Custom Signet-CNN architecture.

In this phase, the visual features that portray the signer's character and mental state are being captured. Every signature possesses individual structural aspects, which are **size, slant, spacing, alignment, and stroke flow**, and these correspond to different personality dimensions. The Signet-CNN framework gets the images that have been preprocessed and passes them through its various layers to the expert who extracts these important visual features.

The **Convolutional Layers** of Signet-CNN are the basic elements in the feature extraction stage. These layers apply small filters to the input images exposing the features such as curves, edges, and textures in a local manner. One of the non-linear activation functions, **ReLU (Rectified Linear Unit)**, allows the network to distinguish even the slightest differences in signature styles. The next **pooling layers** first lower the data's dimensionality and then keep through a process called spatial down ampling only the most significant patterns. This leads to the model consuming less computational power and at the same time the significant visual features being exposed.

The following Figure. 4-3 shows Feature Extraction in proposed Signet-CNN – The depicted image depicts the passing of the input signature image through convolution, ReLU, and pooling layers in the Signet-CNN model, wherein key spatial and structural features for personality classification are extracted.

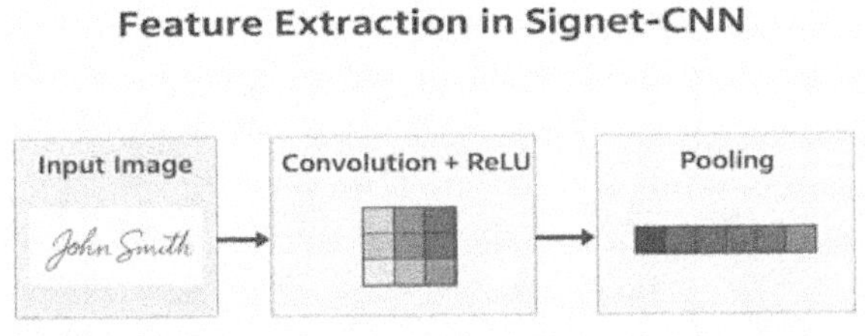

Figure. 4-3 Feature Extraction in Signet-CNN

Through multiple layers of convolution and pooling, the final output goes through the **flattening layer**, which transforms the multidimensional feature maps into a single feature vector. This vector is the summary of all the extracted characteristics of the particular signature and is therefore the input for the classification layers. These features are so effective that they can even depict how the person writes their name—the curves, letter connections, pressure spots, and baseline consistency—all of these being the main personality traits indicators from the literature [1], [14], [38].

The deep learning way that has been adopted for Signet-CNN ensures the extraction of traits that is solely based on the data. This differs from the graphology-based methods that are traditional and constantly apply subjective human interpretation to the whole process, as the CNN system automatically learns to coarsely depict and finely depict the data. That's why it picks up the **low-level details (edges, corners)** and **high-level abstractions (writing style, pressure flow, and signature rhythm)** all at once.

To sum up, the feature extraction stage processes the raw signature images and changes them into very informative feature vectors that are very informative. Afterwards, the extracted features are forwarded to the classification module where the system predicts one of the eight personality types: Analytical, Assertive, Introverted, Sociable, Practical, Optimistic, Creative, or Nervous.The admixture of convolution, activation, pooling, and flattening in the Signet-CNN leads to accurate and strong personality prediction, proving the power of deep learning in the analysis of behavioral pattern [25], [38], [57].

The process of feature extraction is shown in the following Figure.4-4.

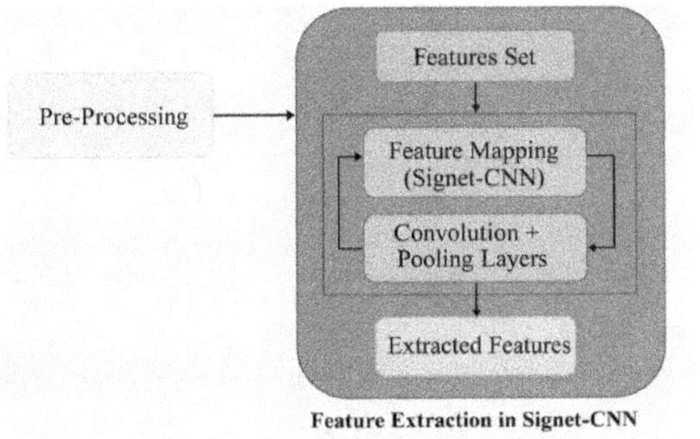

Figure.4-4 Feature extraction

The model follows the Signet-CNN process of extracting the visual characteristics with a weighted rule-based scoring to further the reinforcement of feature-trait relationships. The weights from the rule-based matrix established in the system determine the scores of the visual features, which consist of baseline alignment, slant, size, spacing, and curvature. Each feature has a predefined numerical value that adds up to certain personality traits based on its psychological importance. For example, the rightward slant and high baseline weights indicate being social or optimistic traits, whereas the close letter spacing might imply that the person is an analyzer or introverted, etc. These rules - maintained in the scoring dataset - are very crucial in the conversion of the features acquired from the CNN into interpretable, graphology-based indicators. The introduction of the rule-based scoring not only augments the interpretability of the extracted features thus, making them more reliable, but also prepares them for the classification stage where the final personality prediction will take place [8], [14], [26].

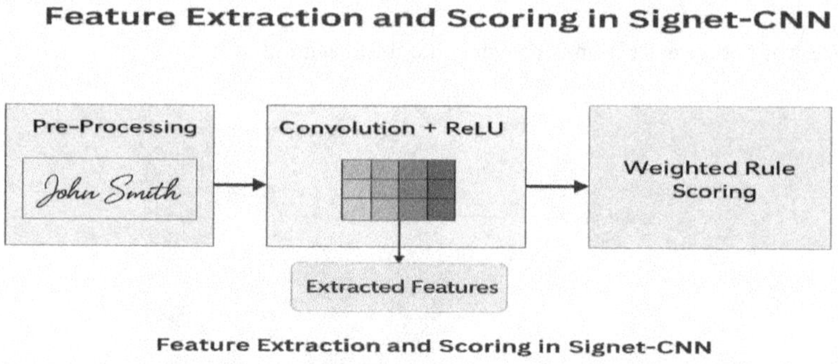

Figure.4-5 Feature Extraction and Weighted Rule-Based Scoring in Signet-CNN

4.2.3 Signature Personality Classification

In the **classification phase**, where the attributes processed are fed into completely interconnected dense layers. The Softmax activation function is used at the final layer to differentiate each signature among **eight personality types**: Analytical, Assertive, Introverted, Sociable, Practical, Optimistic, Creative, and Nervous. The model is further used for **CNN inference testing** during this period, where the trained model is then applied to **live prediction**, which facilitates the real-time personality identification process when a new signature sample is presented.

In this step, the neural network of deep learning interprets the characteristics that were already extracted by Signet-CNN and, furthermore, turns them into predictions that are understandable and connected to the person's traits. This is the stage where the whole system's decision-making layer is formed, which takes the visual features learned and assigns them to a predefined personality category.

The feature vectors that have been extracted are provided by the layers of convolution as well as pooling, and these vectors are then transmitted through a **layer of flattening**. The function of the flattening layer is to transform the feature maps that are of several dimensions into a one-dimensional array that is suitable for being processed by the layers that are fully connected. The characteristics that have been reduced to one dimension contain the most telling details that have been gleaned from the convolutional network, such as the orientation of shapes, slant direction, and spacing patterns, which are the most important in determining the specific personality indicators that are characteristic of the individual.

The features after flattening are then passed to **fully connected dense layers** where high-level reasoning takes place and all the previously extracted patterns get combined. Each neuron of these dense layers gets to learn weighted relationships among features that can make it detect very subtle differences in the behavioral patterns of the signature. The non-linearity is introduced by the **ReLU(Rectified Linear Unit)** activation function, and this makes it possible for the model to learn relationships between the signature traits and the personality types that are very complex.

In order to avoid overfitting, a **dropout layer** is applied which at random times switches off a certain number of the neurons during training. This makes sure the model fits well to the signatures it hasn't seen before and that it also keeps its strength. The **Softmax activation function** is employed by the final dense layer which transforms the output into probability values distributed among the eight personality classes - Analytical, Assertive, Introverted, Sociable, Practical, Optimistic, Creative, and Nervous. The personality type with the highest probability is chosen as the predicted one.

Moreover, a **weighted rule-based scoring mechanism**, which is integrated after feature extraction, is one of the main advantage of the model. The importance (weights) assigned to the features chosen for this scoring aligns with the graphological traits that are predefined and prevalent in the dataset. The combination of deep learning model predictions with these rule-based adjustments improves the interpretability and reliability of the classification results.

The combination of CNN-based learning and rule-based scoring leads to the situation where not only does the system classify signatures in a fast manner, but it also points out the visual attributes that are the most significant ones for the personality dimension of each case. This hybrid model increases accuracy as well as transparency, making it appropriate for psychological analysis, recruitment, and forensic evaluation.

The proposed model guarantees high precision through meticulous training, hyperparameter tuning, and validation. It takes advantage of the power of deep learning in eliminating subjective bias that is usually present in manual graphological analysis and thus, gives out consistent, reliable, and data-driven results.

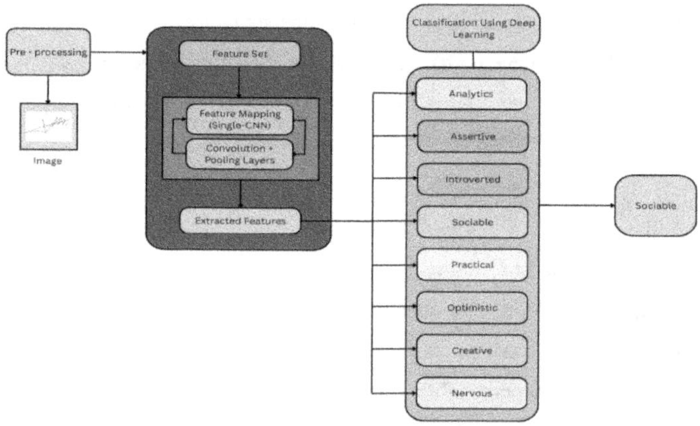

Figure.4-6 personality classification

4.3 Features of proposed model

It's the process that can automatically recognize the different personality traits of people just by looking at their signatures and categorizing them according to their patterns. The model has the following features:

1. **Graphological Trait Integration:**
   Utilizes basic graphological features such as baseline position, size, slope, spacing, and curvature that correspond to different personality traits.
2. **Automated Feature Learning:**
   The Signet-CNN model by itself extracts the complicated spatial and structural patterns from the signature images and thus increases the precision of the features.
3. **Weighted Rule-Based Scoring:**
   The final outcome of high interpretability and prediction accuracy is achieved by the scoring system based on the psychological weights assigned to each trait and the combination of CNN's output and the scoring system.
4. **Robust Preprocessing Framework:**
   Every signature undergoes a series of operations such as resizing, converting to grayscale, and normalizing which not only eliminate the noise but also make the dataset uniform thus aiding effective learning.
5. **Multi-Class Personality Prediction:**
   The algorithm divides the signatures into **eight different personality types**—Analytical, Assertive, Introverted, Sociable, Practical, Optimistic, Creative, and Nervous—thus providing a comprehensive understanding of the characters' behaviors.
6. **End-to-End Deep Learning Pipeline:**
   An entire operation of preprocessing, feature extraction, weighted scoring, and classification is merged into one single fully automated pipeline that not only eases the processing but also makes it more adaptable for the real-time applications.

4.4 Advantages of proposed model

The proposed **Signet-CNN Personality Classification Model** has several advantages that greatly contribute to its performance, reliability, and social applicability:

- **High Accuracy and Reliability:**
  The model provides robust and consistent results through deep feature learning in

conjunction with weighted rule-based refinement thus reducing classification errors significantly as a consequence.

- **Interpretability of Predictions:**
  The combination of graphological weighting and the model is a huge step in the direction of total transparency of predictions as it links every personality selection to easily understandable visual traits.
- **Adaptability and Scalability:**
  The model's structure allows for it to be easily adjusted to new data and also for it to be configured to fit various personality models or handwriting types.
- **Reduced Manual Intervention:**
  Graphological knowledge is not a prerequisite for the analysis procedure since all the processes are automated; however, the analysis is still done with great care.
- **Enhanced Computational Efficiency:**
  The CNN model has been fine-tuned in such a manner that not only fast training and inference are achieved, but also very low power consumption during the processes.
- **Societal and Behavioral Insight:**
  The analysis of the personalities and behaviors of people leads to the discovery of their recruitment, counseling, education, and psychological assessment potentials.
- **Potential for Real-Time Implementation:**
  The model can be incorporated into live systems where the prediction of personality from digital signatures can be done in tandem with the personality prediction organizational or security documentation. It allows for interactions and makes the machine sympathetic and feel like a human.

4.5 Application of Proposed model

The **Signature-Based Personality Classification Model** that has been proposed is going to be applicable to various sectors where personality insights can be made to support decision-making process. The system can find its application in such areas as:

- **Recruitment and Human Resource Management:**
  The model is going to be of assistance to the employers in the process of judging by means of signature, the candidates' behavioral tendencies and personality fit altogether with the support of traditional psychometric assessments.
- **Educational Guidance and Counseling:**
  By the counseling process, the model can help the counselor in regard to the understanding of the learning styles of the students, their confidence levels, and their creativity, thus, they can be directed to the right career or academic path.
- **Behavioural Analytics and Consumer Research:**
  The personality classification can be one of the tools for businesses that can help them gain insight into consumer attitudes, preferences, and decision-making patterns thus facilitating marketing and service personalization.
- **Career and Personal Development:**
  Individuals may refer to the feedback of the model with a view to recognizing their strengths and the areas they can improve in, which would lead to personal growth and increased performance at work.
- **Studies on Societal Behavior and Policy Making:**
  The broader setting makes it possible for researchers and policymakers in personality data to monitor and analyze the trends of the collective behavior of the society which can later be effectively utilized in the development of social programs and community initiatives.

4.6 Summary

This chapter illustrates the Signature-Based Personality Classification Model that has been proposed, along with its overall system design and architecture. It elaborates the main components, which are the preprocessing module, the Signet-CNN model for feature extraction, weighted rule-based scoring, and personality classification. Also, chapter points out the main features, advantages, and applications of this proposed model.

Chapter-5
Implementation of Proposed Model

Chapter 5: Implementation of the Proposed Model

This chapter provides detail implementation of the proposed Signature-Based Personality Classification Model that uses deep learning methods. It gives thorough explanation of the model's modules and demonstrates how the system processes signature images for personality trait classification. The implementation gives priority to the creation of the unique Signet-CNN structure for automatic feature extraction and personality prediction.

5.1 Introduction

The proposed Classification model runs in Anaconda environment with Python 3.10. Jupyter Notebook is the tool selected to load, preprocess, and divide the dataset of 601 signature images into training and testing sets. The custom Signet-CNN architecture built on TensorFlow and Keras is the one being used to design, train, and validate the model. OpenCV is used for the image preprocessing and enhancing procedure that is aimed at guaranteeing the same quality and standard. The experiments are done on a system that is made up of Windows 11 (64-bit) os with 16 GB RAM ,TensorFlow with GPU support for faster calculations.

5.2 Implementation of proposed model

The proposed signature-based personality classification model has been developed using Python in Jupyter Notebook through Anaconda. Anaconda is a distribution of Python that is open-source and offers a unified platform for all the three categories of research—machine learning, deep learning, and data science—all at the same time. It eliminates all the hassles related to the model development by merging the three critical aspects of model development into one platform that is package management, library installation, and environment configuration.

Python is the top-leading programming language in the computer vision and image processing industry due to its versatility. The model built on deep learning is the main area of its application due to the simplicity, flexibility, and great support for scientific computing provided by Python. Python has been employed in this model to create, train, and assess the Signet-CNN model for personality recognition based on signature photographs.

The incorporation of Anaconda in the deep learning research has made the working environment very favorable due to its offer of features such as built-in libraries, Jupyter Notebook integration, and compatibility with TensorFlow and Keras frameworks. It ensures proper maintenance of dependencies for model reproducibility and performance through stable and flexible ecosystem for managing multiple environments.

5.2.1 Data set

Quality and variety of the dataset are the cornerstones of deep learning model. For the purpose of this research, a custom dataset comprising 601 digital signature images are developed for the training and evaluation of the proposed Signature-Based Personality Classification Model (Signet-CNN). Each signature in this dataset is a distinctive blend of personal traits, writing patterns, and stylistic tendons that are the psychological characteristics of the signer. The dataset is thoroughly prepared, annotated, and organized to provide a balanced representation of all the personality classes defined.

5.2.1.1 Dataset Overview

The dataset includes high-resolution digital signature images taken from people of various ages, genders, and professional backgrounds in order to obtain the most natural variation in handwriting patterns. Each sample is collected in image format, either .jpg or .png, and the methods used were scanning of physical signatures. The images differ very slightly in terms of angle, pressure, and texture of the writing surface — these are the factors that contribute to real-world variability which is a must for creating a robust model.

Each image corresponds to one of **eight personality categories** defined in the system:

1. Analytical
2. Assertive
3. Introverted
4. Sociable
5. Practical
6. Optimistic
7. Creative
8. Nervous

Above personality category represents a different type of behavior, thus it makes it easier for the deep learning model to understand minute differences among the signatures of different people.

The following Figure 5.1 shows Sample Signature Images.

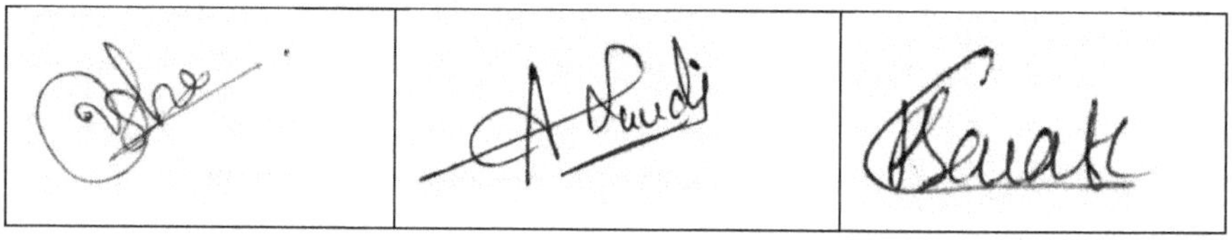

Figure 5.1: Sample Signature Images from the Dataset

5.2.1.2 Data Annotation and Labeling

The data collection is followed by a systematic annotation process for each image. The marking of each signature is done based on graphological heuristics and using the personality indicators as reference points, namely stroke size, slant, pressure consistency, spacing, curvature, and alignment. These characteristics of signature patterns have long been associated with psychological traits in graphology[22][51][87]. For example:

- The above-mentioned traits of personality and character—sociability and optimism—are often represented through **right slant** and **wide spacing[34][12].**
- **Heavy pressure** combined with firm strokes is linked to assertiveness and confidence.

- Analytical or introverted nature is often inferred from **small, compact signatures[6].**
- **Irregular alignment** or inconsistent flow may reflect nervousness or instability[56].

The dataset realizes both psychological validity and structural balance by incorporating these concepts in the labeling process.

5.2.1.3 Data Organization and Structure

The dataset is systematically organized into separate folders for each personality trait, ensuring clear distinction and ease of access during model training. The structure is as follows:

```
Dataset/
├── Analytical/
├── Assertive/
├── Introverted/
├── Sociable/
├── Practical/
├── Optimistic/
├── Creative/
└── Nervous/
```

Each folder contains nearly equal number of images, ensuring balanced class distribution to avoid bias during model training. This uniformity helps the network generalize well across all personality types instead of overfitting to dominant classes.

5.2.1.4 Preprocessing and Standardization

Because the signature images varied in size, orientation, and background, the first preprocessing is applied to make them uniform and suitable for model training. Using **OpenCV** and **NumPy**, the following steps are performed:

- **Resizing:** All signature images are resized to 128×128 pixels so they match the required input size for the CNN model.
- **Grayscale Conversion:** Images are converted from RGB to grayscale, reducing computational complexity while preserving important texture and edge details.

- **Normalization:** After that, the pixel values are scaled between 0 and 1. This helps the model learn faster and makes the training process more stable.
- **Noise removal:** Gaussian and median filtering algorithms are used to reduce background noise or scanning related artifacts.
- **Edge Enhancement:** Canny edge detection is adopted in cases where improvements in sharpness of stroke patterns is needed.

This preprocessing pipeline, standardize the images to high-quality inputs suitable for CNN feature extraction.

The following Figure 5.2 shows Preprocessing Function for Signature Images in Signet-CNN.

```
# Preprocessing function
def preprocess_signature(image_path, save_path):
    img = cv2.imread(image_path)
    # Convert to grayscale
    gray = cv2.cvtColor(img, cv2.COLOR_BGR2GRAY)
    # Resize to fixed dimensions (128x128)
    resized = cv2.resize(gray, (128, 128))
    # Gaussian blur for noise reduction
    blurred = cv2.GaussianBlur(resized, (3, 3), 0)
    # Normalize pixel values to range [0,1]
    normalized = blurred / 255.0
    # Save preprocessed image
    cv2.imwrite(save_path, (normalized * 255).astype(np.uint8))

# Apply preprocessing to all images
for folder in os.listdir(input_dir):
    folder_path = os.path.join(input_dir, folder)
    save_folder = os.path.join(output_dir, folder)
    os.makedirs(save_folder, exist_ok=True)

    for file in os.listdir(folder_path):
        img_path = os.path.join(folder_path, file)
        save_path = os.path.join(save_folder, file)
        preprocess_signature(img_path, save_path)
```

Figure 5.2: Preprocessing Function for Signature Images in Signet-CNN

The data collection and preprocessing phase yields well-annotated dataset for training a deep learning-based personality classification system. The quality and balance of the dataset at this stage promotes the efficient learning of discriminative visual patterns from the signature images; and, subsequently led to accurate feature extraction and confidence in personality prediction stages.

5.2.1.5 Dataset Split

To accurately train and assess the proposed Signet-CNN model, a 3-way split of the dataset is done:

- **Training Set (80%):** used to train the CNN on personality patterns
- **Validation Set (10%):** used to inform model hyperparameter tuning and prevent overfitting
- **Testing Set (10%):** used to assess the accuracy and generalization of the final model.

The three-way split stratified by personality class ensures that each personality class is equivalently represented over all subsets, adding reliability and removing bias in evaluating the model.

In summary, a dataset with 601 annotated signature images is created for accurate and applicable personality classification. The dataset is organized; an appropriate standardized preprocessing method is used for facilitating consistent feature extraction.

5.2.2 Implementation of the proposed Signet-CNN model

The proposed model named **Signet-CNN** has deep learning architecture designed to classify personality based on signatures. The system automatically estimate latent psychological constructs from digital signatures or images of signature by quantifying visual characteristics such as curvature, pressure, alignment, spacing, and rhythm. The Signet-CNN model is implemented in the **TensorFlow–Keras** framework in the **Python 3.10 Anaconda** environment, where **Jupyter Notebook** is used to run experiments on the system. Jupyter Notebook provides an interactive environment where we can visualize in real-time, troubleshoot, and assess models.

The Signet-CNN network has convolutional network structure that supports hierarchical feature learning and stable and consistent classification layers that map visual features into the following eight personality traits: **analytical, assertive, introverted, sociable, practical, optimistic, creative and nervous.**

The model is designed for interpretability, efficiency, and adaptability to small datasets, which is often a limitation in behavioral data collection.

The following Figure 5.3 shows the implementation architecture of the proposed Signet-CNN model.

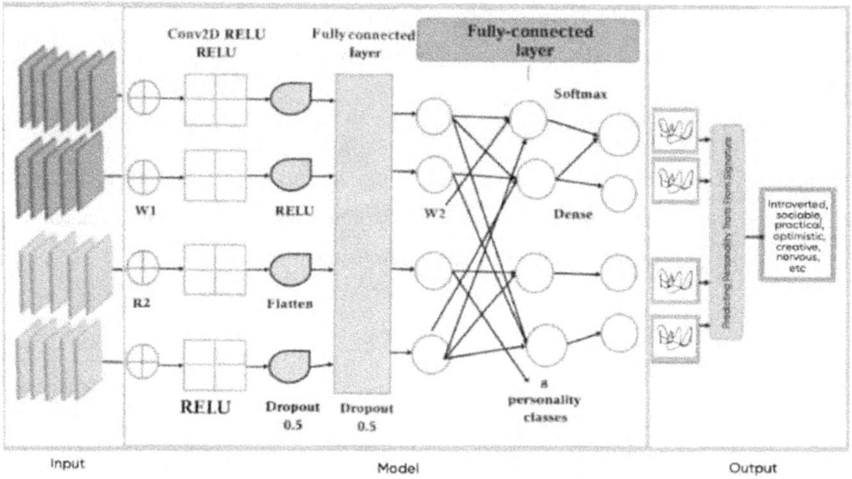

Figure 5.3 shows the implementation architecture of the proposed Signet-CNN model

The Signet-CNN model has three main parts:

1. **Convolutional Layers – Feature Extraction:**
   These layers capture important properties of the signature images including curves, strokes, and textural information through learnable filters.
2. **Pooling Layers - Dimensionality Reduction:**
   Pooling layers merges local feature information and reduces computation by conveying the most important features.

3. **Fully connected layers – Personality Prediction:**

   The fully connected layers take all the features extracted from the previous two layers and use them to classify the signature into one of the personality category.

5.2.2.1 Workflow and Operational Flow

The entire workflow starts with a preprocessed signature image as input, usually resized to 128 × 128 pixels and normalized between 0 and 1. Each image goes through the steps of convolution, activation, and pooling operations sequentially and then the feature representations are passed through a series of dense layers to produce the final classification.

Step-wise Workflow:

1. Input Signature Image
2. Convolution Operations using 3 × 3 filters
3. ReLU Activation Function
4. Pooling Operation (2 × 2 Max Pooling)
5. Flattening Feature Maps
6. Dense Layers for Feature Integration
7. Softmax Output for Personality Prediction

This learning process is applied in a sequential manner so that the model can develop low-level stroke edges to high-level stylistic interpretation.

5.2.2.2 Detailed Description of Layers

a. Convolutional Layers

Every convolutional layer applies a collection of trainable kernels (3 × 3 filters) that slide over the signature image to extract local patterns. The first layer detect the most basic shapes and edges, while many of the other layers combine those features and develop more advanced elements, e.g. curves, loops, pressure fluctuations, and alignment tendencies.

The model is comprised of three convolutional blocks, arranged as follows:

- **Conv2D (32 filters, ReLU)** - finds basic edges, pen-lifts, and simple directional strokes.
- **Conv2D (64 filters, ReLU)** - finds curvature flow, depth of pressure, and continuity of strokes.
- **Conv2D (128 filters, ReLU)** - finds advanced in high-level style patterns such as symmetry, spacing rhythm, and overall signature balance.

Mathematically, each convolution is expressed as:

$$f(i,j) = \sum_{m=0}^{M-1} \sum_{n=0}^{N-1} I(i+m, j+n)\, K(m,n)$$

In the equation, input patch K indicates the kernel, and f(i,j) denotes the activation associated with a neuron.

The **ReLU (Rectified Linear Unit)** activation function performs the non-linear transformation.

$$\mathrm{ReLU}(x) = \max(0, x)$$

which denotes non-linearity in the gradient, avoids vanishing gradient problems and speeds up convergence. The output of the convolution, or **feature maps**, represent an upstream and downstream encoding of visual hierarchies: early layers describe line observables, while lowest level layers are compositional features that capture a wide range of features linked to personality in a stylistic manner.

The following Figure 5.4 shows Feature Extraction and Pooling Process in Signet-CNN.

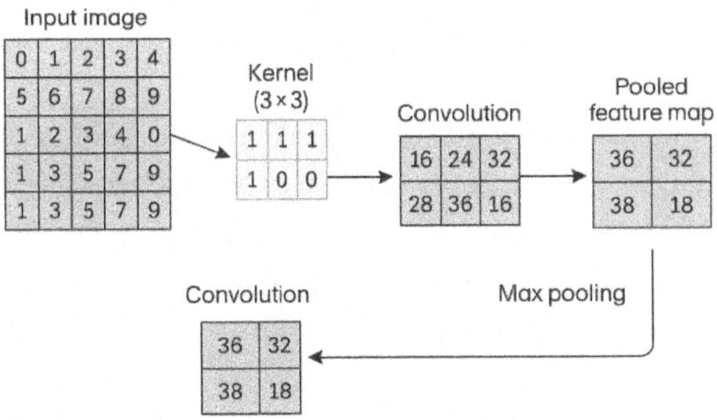

Figure 5.4 Feature Extraction and Pooling Process in Signet-CNN

b. Pooling Layers

After each convolution operation, down sampling of the feature maps is performed using the Max Pooling layer with a 2 × 2 window shape. There are three main purposes for pooling:

1. It decreases dimensionality and computational cost.
2. It establishes translation invariance to small spatial variations.
3. It reduces overfitting by retaining the most important features.

The output of the pooling layer, P(x,y) for a window size of m×n, is calculated by:

$$P(x, y) = \max_{0 \leq i < m,\, 0 \leq j < n} f(x + i, y + j)$$

Pooling maintains the most informative areas from the signature such as stroke crossings and curvature inflections points which are important features for examining a signature in graphology.

c. Fully Connected and Classification Layers

Following the convolutional hierarchy, the Flatten layer transform 2-D feature maps into a 1-D feature vector. This can be followed by two dense layers:

- **Dense (128 neurons, ReLU) :** learns high-level interactions between features that have been extracted (e.g. Line spacing and angle in combination may demonstrate confidence or introversion).
- **Dense (8 neurons, Softmax) :** performs the multiclass personality classification task.

To minimize overfitting and for better generalization of the model, **Dropout layers (rate = 0.5)** is included between the dense layers, randomly deactivating neurons during training.

The **Softmax** activiation function is then applied at output layer. The Softmax function will transform the raw outputs into class probabilities:

$$P(y_i) = \frac{e^{z_i}}{\sum_{j=1}^{8} e^{z_j}}$$

Note there will be a sum of the probability with respect to the 8 personality traits of 1 (i.e. 100%), which will correspond to the predicted personality trait.

The following Figure 5.5 shows Convolutional and Fully Connected Layers of Signet-CNN.

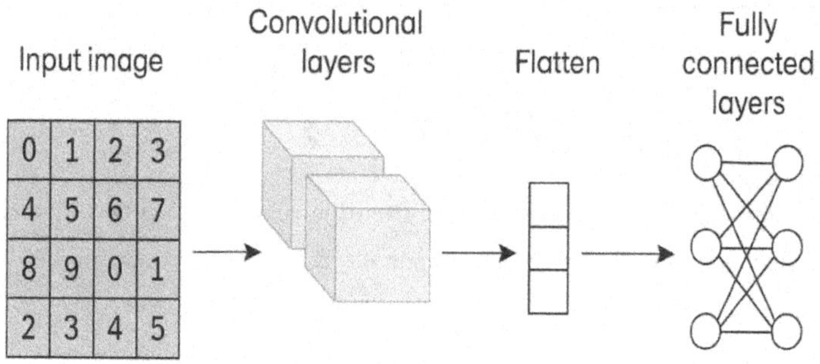

Figure 5.5 Convolutional and Fully Connected Layers of Signet-CNN

5.2.2.3 Model Compilation and Training Configuration

The Signet-CNN model is compiled with:

- **Optimizer chosen:** Adaptive Moment Estimation(ADAM), which can adapt the learning-rate in the optimization problem by maintaining momentum which allows faster convergence.
- **Loss Function:** Categorical Cross-Entropy, the loss function is applicable for multi-class personality prediction.
- **Batch Size** of 32 samples per iteration.
- **Epochs:** 20-35 depending on the stability of the validation.

The training-validation split of 80:20 is used for ensuring reliable generalizability, along with data augmentation (zoom, rotation, shear, horizontal flip) is used for simulating natural writer variation in signature writing; which increase robustness.

The following Figure 5.6 shows the Code in TensorFlow–Keras

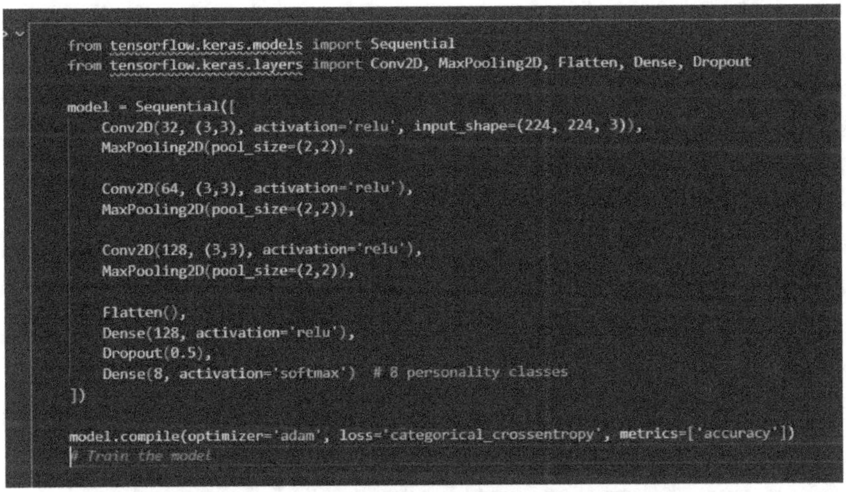

```
from tensorflow.keras.models import Sequential
from tensorflow.keras.layers import Conv2D, MaxPooling2D, Flatten, Dense, Dropout

model = Sequential([
    Conv2D(32, (3,3), activation='relu', input_shape=(224, 224, 3)),
    MaxPooling2D(pool_size=(2,2)),

    Conv2D(64, (3,3), activation='relu'),
    MaxPooling2D(pool_size=(2,2)),

    Conv2D(128, (3,3), activation='relu'),
    MaxPooling2D(pool_size=(2,2)),

    Flatten(),
    Dense(128, activation='relu'),
    Dropout(0.5),
    Dense(8, activation='softmax')  # 8 personality classes
])

model.compile(optimizer='adam', loss='categorical_crossentropy', metrics=['accuracy'])
# Train the model
```

Figure 5.6 Model Implementation Code in TensorFlow–Keras

5.2.2.4 Learning Dynamics and Interpretation

During training, automatically filters adjust to detect visual signals that are associated with behavioral tendencies:

Signature Pattern	Behavioral Interpretation
High pressure and compact strokes	Assertive and goal-oriented
Large spacing and smooth flow	Sociable and open-minded
Sharp angles and rigid lines	Analytical and critical
Uneven slant and breaks in flow	Nervous or emotionally unstable
Continuous curves and looped letters	Creative and intuitive
Uniform height and balanced proportion	Practical and disciplined

Table.5-1 Signature Patterns and Their Behavioral Interpretations

Above Table 5.1 shows different signature patterns and their corresponding behavioral interpretations grouped together. The table indicates a link between some signature characteristics, like the pressure applied, spacing between letters, angles formed, slant, and the overall structure, and personality types that range from boldness and inventiveness through emotional instability and logical reasoning to the opposite ends of the spectrum.

Each convolution filter strengthens learning of the micro-patterns. **Backpropagation** is used to iteratively modify the filter weights to reduce the classification error. The gradient of the loss is updated as follows for each weight wij:

$$w_{ij}^{(t+1)} = w_{ij}^{(t)} - \eta \frac{\partial L}{\partial w_{ij}}$$

where η represents the learning rate and LLL is the categorical cross-entropy loss.

As the model converges, its internal feature maps develop into highly discriminative abstractions that separate small differences between traits.

5.2.2.5 *Model Architecture Summary*

Component	Description
Input	128 × 128 preprocessed signature image
Convolution Layers	3 (32, 64, 128 filters, 3×3 kernels)
Pooling Layers	3 (2×2 Max Pooling)
Dense Layers	128 ReLU + 8 Softmax
Dropout Rate	0.5 (for regularization)
Optimizer	Adam (Adaptive Momentum)
Loss Function	Categorical Cross-Entropy
Output Classes	8 Personality Traits
Environment	Python 3.10, Anaconda, TensorFlow–Keras

Table.5-2 CNN Model Architecture Configuration

The architectural components and configurations used in the proposed Signet-CNN model are elaborated in Table 5.2. The specification of inputs, convolution–pooling structure, dense layer configuration, dropout rate, and optimization strategy are all clearly outlined, in addition to the dataset environment. All these aspects combined characterize the entire model pipeline that has been developed for the purpose of classifying signatures into eight distinct personality traits categories.

This architecture enhances the capacity of the model to learn local micro-strokes and global spatial relationships, while maintaining efficiency in computation. The three Convolutional blocks succeeded in finding a balance between depth and generalization and are able to train on a reasonable size dataset of 601 signature samples.

5.2.2.6 Interpretation and Generalization

Post-training, the Softmax output layer produces probability distributions for each of the personality classes. As an example, a sample prediction may yield:

Trait	Probability
Analytical	0.05
Assertive	0.62
Introverted	0.03
Sociable	0.10
Practical	0.06
Optimistic	0.04
Creative	0.08
Nervous	0.02

Table 5.3 Predicted Personality Trait Probabilities

The model-generates predicted probability distribution as shown in Table 5.3 for the the eight-personality traits for a particular signature sample. The output reveals 'Assertive' as the most likely trait with the highest probability indicating it to be the most characteristic quality, whereas the traits of Sociable and Creative have been given moderate probabilities close to one another, while the rest are rated rather low. Thus, this distribution can be seen as the model's evaluation of the signature's behavior patterns.

Assertive is the chosen final classification in this example.

The distribution also adds interpretability - a higher secondary probability could indicate a mixed tendency for that personality, rather than being predicated exclusively on a single dominant trait.

The **Signet-CNN** model seamlessly converts visual signature data into quantifiable representations of personality properties. Via a layered structure consisting of convolution, pooling, dense, and softmax layers, the model enables various levels of abstraction through raw image pixels to psychological meaning.
Through the building of deep features, intensive optimization, and scoring tabulations, Signet-CNN achieves an effective data-driven approach to revealing human personality via digital signatures.

5.2.3 Feature extraction and Scoring

The **feature extraction and scoring phase** is the analytical heart of the proposed **Signet-CNN** model. This phase rips the formatted signature images into well-defined and organized numerical representations, and ultimately exposes valuable behavioral patterning. Signet-CNN utilizes different convolution and pooling layers to produce combinations of spatial, structural, and stylistic clues to defend each classification of the signer's individual personality constructs. There is also a **weight-based rule score**, grounded in graphology and heuristics drawn from slant, size, pressure, & stroke continuity to reinforce the deep learning model classification.

5.2.3.1 Feature Extraction Using Signet-CNN

The extraction of the features will take place following the preprocessing of the signature image — resized, normalized, and converted into grayscale. The image will be passed through a stack of convolutional layers that learn feature hierarchies. The early convolutional layers will learn **low-level features** such as edges and curves, but deeper layers will learn **high-level abstractions**, such as stroke pressure variance, alignment, and rhythm of writing.

Each convolutional layer will use a number of filters of size **3 × 3** to scan across the image matrix. The filters act as detectors for the detection of specific stroke orientations and directional textures, while the **Rectified Linear Unit (ReLU)** activation brings non-linearity and allows predictions to distinguish subtle aspects of writing. The outputs of the filters are **feature maps** that define abstraction for specific attributes from the signature.

The mathematical representation of the convolution operation is:

$$F(x,y) = (I * K)(x,y) = \sum_m \sum_n I(x-m, y-n) \cdot K(m,n)$$

where I(x, y) represents the input image, and **K(m, n)** is the convolution kernel (filter).

This produces a feature map, F(x, y), that broadens the regions in which a certain pattern (e.g., a curve or an upward slant) is most prominent. Each layer of convolution is then followed by a **MaxPooling2D** operation which reduces the spatial dimension based on selecting the maximal value in the filter window (often 2×2). This layer serves to increases translational invariance, in other words, if the stroke of the signature shifts slightly, the feature extracted will be invariant. The pooling layer also helps to avoid overfitting and to speed up computation as it reduces the number of parameters which must be trained.

The following are stages of convolution, activation, and pooling which take place in the proposed model.

The feature maps of each layer represent the signature in a hierarchical manner:

- **First convolutional block:** Identifies simple curves, loops, and intersections.
- **Second block:** Looks for thickness, stratification of pressure, and location confidence.
- **Third block:** Identifies more complex structural features as baseline flow, cadence of strokes, and regularity of space.

The final convolutional and pooling layers turn the multi-dimension feature maps into a single-dimension feature vector in which all properties of the signature are retained in a numerical format.

5.2.3.2 Weighted Rule-Based Scoring Mechanism

To further interpretability and definitiveness, a **Weighted Rule-Based Scoring System** is introduced after feature extraction. The scoring mechanism evaluates the specific structural and stylistic features extracted from the CNN layers and gives **weighted scores** to each feature based on established graphological principles.

Each of the features that are extracted represents one or more of the eight personality traits: **Analytical, Assertive, Introverted, Sociable, Practical, Optimistic, Creative, and Nervous.**

This combined model is interpretable and accurate in its predictive capability. Although the CNN layers learnt the features end to end, the weighted rule-based scoring provides decision logic that stays close to graphological principles and matching predictions to those principles. Overall, these two aspects of the model enable the proposed model to monitor variances in the nuanced characteristics of the signature and provide reliable predictions for the personality profiles.

5.2.5 Analysis of feature extraction & Classification

The feature extraction component of the proposed Signet-CNN model explains the process of identification and processing of salient signature features to classify personality. The model extracts specific geometric and structural features such as curve form, alignment, pressure strength, and spacing between strokes. These are learned features indicating the signer's writing rhythm, control, and consistency, which represent behavioral and cognitive tendencies relating to personality.

Signet-CNN uses convolutional layers to capture spatial information in multiple levels or hierarchy. The earliest layers identify primitive components of the signature, such as stroke direction, edges, and corners, while the deeper convolutional layers identify beyond, recognizing abstract features, such as flow and coherence to indicate rhythm and balance. For compressing the information, pooling layers are also included, which helps cut down redundancy, while retaining the key information. Employing multiple calculations in the feature extraction stage increases the chances of identifying subtle changes in stroke or curve that are often psychologically meaningful.

After these features have been extracted, the fully-connected layers accomplish the classification task. The flattened feature maps take into account different configurational relationships regarding the separate attributes of the signature. Each neuron in each of the dense layers is linked with a combination of visual and behavioral attributes that are learned during training. **A Weighted Rule Based Scoring Mechanism** is added to refine predictions by returning weights to defining attributes - such as, line pressure, spacing reliability, or angularity

Kamrol et al. [80] (HMM)	91.30	90.80	91.00
Proposed Signet-CNN Model	**97.17**	**96.31**	**96.85**

Table 6-3. Comparison of Performance Metrics with Existing Works

The proposed model demonstrates the **highest precision of 97.17%, recall of 96.31%**, and **F1-score of 96.85%**, surpassing earlier approaches in all three metrics. This improvement can be attributed to the optimized convolutional layers and efficient feature extraction tailored for **signature-based personality traits**, which ensures minimal misclassification among personality categories. The balance between precision and recall confirms the model's ability to correctly identify personality classes while maintaining robustness against false predictions. Overall, the **Signet-CNN model** delivers superior consistency and interpretability, outperforming previous deep learning and hybrid models in both recognition accuracy and computational efficiency

Large values for **accuracy, precision**, and **recall** suggest that the Signet-CNN successfully detects distinguishing graphical features in signatures — stroke patterns and curvature along spatial flow and correctly maps them to their underlying descriptive personality categories. The **confusion matrix** provides additional evidence that the predictions align with the unique class underlying distinct signature classifications — highlighting model consistency and robustness across a variety of signature samples.

The following Figure.6-5 indications Confusion Matrix of the proposed model.

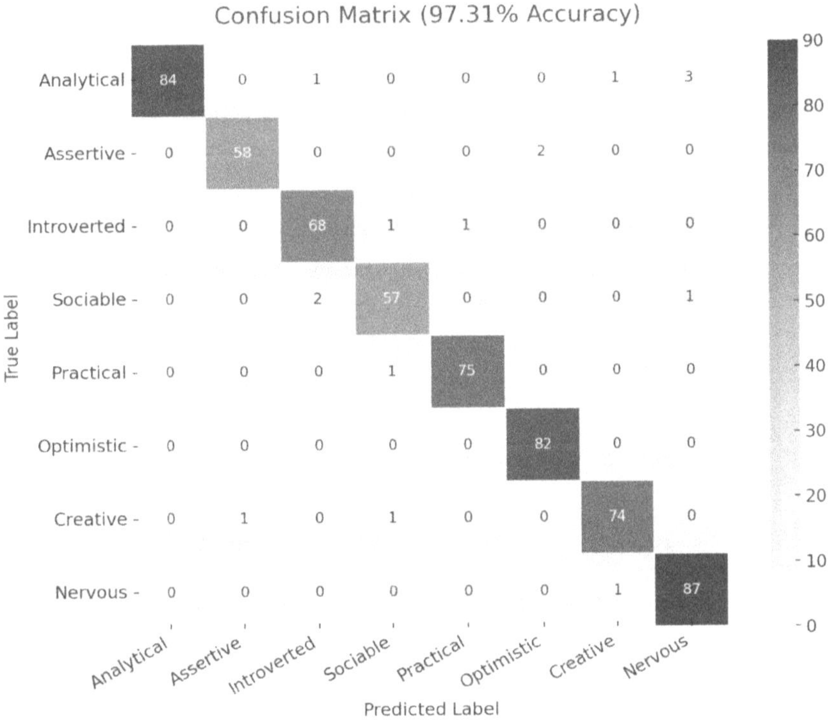

Figure 6-5 Confusion Matrix of Signet Model

The confusion matrix presented in Figure 6.5 shows the class-wise performance of the proposed **Signet-CNN** model toward signature-based personality classification, which achieves **97.31%** overall **accuracy** in predicting personality traits across the eight classes. Each value along the diagonal represents the total samples lying correctly in its particular classification, signaling that most of the predicted personality traits are correct according to the actual personality trait label. For example, the traits **Optimistic (82)**, **Nervous (87)**, and **Practical (75)** indicates the highest predicted count, whereas slight misclassifications happened between the similar behavioral categories, **Introverted** and **Sociable**, where relatives of writing style may be relevant. Overall,

- **Weighted Rule-Based Scoring Integration:**

  The hybrid method combines the predictions made by both the CNN and the rule-based scoring method. This allows to model to refine the results even finer by awarding weights based on graphological heuristics thus enhancing interpretability and trust in classification.

- **Dense Connectivity for Robust Learning:**

  The stratified architecture of the network guarantees the gradient to flow efficiently and the features to be reused, thus minimizing the possibility of vanishing gradients and, at the same time, speeding up the convergence of the model during the training process.

- **Optimized for Limited Data:**

  The model is able to cope with training very well even with the small datasets (601 signature images), while transfer learning and regularization are helping to further its generalization ability.

- **Explainable Predictions:**

  The combination of visual feature maps with weighted rule-based refinement provides a clear view of the decision-making process and this makes the system appropriate for HR analytics, behavioral research, and forensic interpretation.

7.3 Performance evaluation of proposed model

The performance metrics and computational parameters reveal that the **Signet-CNN** model's accuracy, consistency, and robustness in classification of personality from signatures have been establish through rigorous analysis. The process of analysis explored how the model obtained the most distinguishing features of the signatures and how it related those features to the correct personality traits.

The performance metrics that were used to analyse the model is below:

- **Accuracy:**
  This is the ratio of correct predictions of the personality traits to total predictions. The proposed Signet-CNN realized an overall accuracy of **97.31%** through its reliability and precision.

- **Precision:**
  It reflects the ratio of true positives to the number of predicted positives which the model confirms as making fewer false-positive predictions in the case of distinguishing similar signature patterns. The Proposed model has 97.17% Precision.

- **Recall:**
  It helps to find out how effectively the model gets all true positive samples from each personality class, so that no major category is missed. The Proposed model has 96.31% Recall.

- **F1-Score:**
  It represents the harmonic mean of precision and recall, reflects the balance between these two key measures of classification performance. The proposed model has **F1-score of 96.85%**, proving it has stability in complex data scenarios.

- **Confusion Matrix:**

  This summarizes the prediction accuracy per class and also reveals the misclassification patterns for the eight personality traits—Analytical, Assertive, Introverted, Sociable, Practical, Optimistic, Creative, and Nervous. The values in confusion matrix prove that the majority of predictions are made accurately according to their real labels, and that there is very little overlap between the closely related personality types.

- **Computation Efficiency:**
  The lightweight CNN model guarantees quicker training and also less memory usage with

the same degree of accuracy. Thus, it is possible to process the signatures in real time and also to get personality predictions very quickly.

- **Model Scalability and Robustness:**

  The Signet-CNN architecture is very efficient in generalizing to new and unseen signatures by combining the stages of preprocessing, feature extraction, and scoring.

- **Interpretability and Transparency:**

  The model is able to give explanations for its predictions based on the combined effect of CNN-based feature learning and rule-based weighted scoring. In other words, every classification can be related to specific aspects of the signature such as stroke patterns, line pressure, or spatial distribution.

In conclusion, the Proposed Signet-CNN that has been presented is a model that has **a very good balance of accuracy, interpretability,** and **computational efficiency**. Moreover, the use of **weighted scoring refinement** increases its ability to tell apart very slight graphological differences between personality traits that are alike.

7.4 Advantage of the model

The proposed signature-based personality classification model has number of advantages as listed below:

- **High accuracy and robustness:** The Signet-CNN model reaches a remarkable 97.31% accuracy, which is a clear indication of its reliability and consistency in classifying all the eight personality types.

- **Flexibility and scalability:** The model is not only easy to adapt for bigger datasets but can also be combined with other biometric traits for future research.

- **Efficient feature learning:** The model through convolution and weighted scoring techniques, captures the differences in signature strokes, and pressure and spacing which in turn enhances the precision of the classification.

- **Reduced manual intervention:** The automated feature extraction done by the model gets rid of the traditional graphological assessment which results in objectivity and quicker analysis.

- **Improved decision-making:** The model helps psychologists, recruiters, and forensic experts make more informed choices by offering clear, data-based insights into a person's personality traits.

- **Enhanced interpretability:** The model's transparency has been improved by the weighted rule-based scoring system that links the visual patterns extracted to the personality tendencies.

- **Real-time applicability:** The lightweight CNN architecture trained and predicted quickly for the deployment in the real-world systems like HR analytics or behavioral profiling.

7.5 Applications of the model

The model can be utilized in various different areas such as recruitment and human resource management, educational guidance, counseling, forensic, mental health, and emotional well-being, behavioral analytics, and consumer research, career, and personal development as well as societal behavior studies and policymaking.

The following are applications of where the model can be applied:

- Identifying and measuring personality traits during recruitments and employee's evaluation.
- Giving candidates and students guidance of their career and education according to their personality type.

- Screening mental and emotional health through the monitoring of behavior patterns.
- Strengthening the analysis of consumer and behavioral research.
- Aiding in the making of policies that concern human behavior and social dynamics.
- Delivering personality insights automatically to improve the counseling process.

7.6 Limitations of the model

The **Signature-Based Personality Classification Model** that is based on signatures is an effective one that can spot human characteristics through signature images with the help of deep learning.

Nonetheless, there are still some restrictions that define the limits of the present work:

- The model only analyzes the **signature's visual features** and does not use any other behavioral data such as handwriting dynamics or pressure applied by the stylus.
- It opts for the **static-image method**.

7.7 Future scope

The limitations on the use of the signature in personality classification are a sign of the great potential for the further development of this field.

The next steps of research can be as such:

- Creating a **multimodal method** that integrates still signature images with dynamic handwriting or stylus-motion data to record minuscule behavioral differences.
- Taking the system to **a learning model** that is **independent** of the person, allowing it to generalize well across people with writing styles that are different from each other.
- Implementing preprocessing that is **noise-tolerant** and using **advanced augmentation methods** to cope with the low-quality or distorted signatures.

- **Explainable AI (XAI)** methods may be applied to reveal and clarify which personality-related features the CNN identifies and relies on for its predictions.
- Exploring **hybrid deep learning approaches** that connect CNN with transformer-based models for better feature representation.

7.8 Summary

This chapter summarizes the proposed model Signet CNN with its objectives, features, performance evaluation, advantages, applications, limitations. Moreover, it gives future direction of work to be done in this area of signature analysis.

www.ingramcontent.com/pod-product-compliance
Lightning Source LLC
LaVergne TN
LVHW021736071126
851857LV00040B/1457
* 9 7 9 8 1 8 2 7 3 2 3 3 8 *